NAVAJO TEXTILE ARTS

NAVAJO

TEXTILE ARTS

H. P. MERA

ADDITIONS

BY ROGER AND JEAN MOSS

➜ Peregrine Smith, Inc.
SANTA BARBARA AND SALT LAKE CITY
1975

Library of Congress CIP Information

Mera, Harry Percival, 1875-1951.
   Navajo textile arts.

   Reprint of the 1947 ed. published by
Laboratory of Anthropology, Santa Fe,
N.M.; with new introd.
   1. Navaho Indians—Textile industry
and fabrics. 2. Indians of North America
—Southwest, New—Textile industry and
fabrics. I. Title.
E99.N3M518 1975   746.1'4'0979   75-16296
ISBN 0-87905-040-3

Manufactured in the United States of America

ACKNOWLEDGMENTS

WE would like acknowledge the help and support offered us by a number of people as we undertook the Afterword to this new edition. Our special thanks go to David Noble of the School of American Research for permission to reprint the book, for his help in locating a copy of the rare first edition from which this edition could be made, and for his many helpful suggestions about our text; to Gilbert S. Maxwell for his unique and useful comments; to Dave Fredrickson of Sonoma State College and Vera Mae Fredrickson of Lowie Museum of Anthropology for their careful reading of the text; and to Barbara Busch of Lowie Museum of Anthropology for the information we have received from her in many conversations on Navajo weaving. For the new photographs we would like to thank Marriam Ring, William G. Webb, and José Gutierrez. Textiles used in new photographs are from private collections, and we are grateful to the owners for allowing us to use them.

Roger and Jean Moss

CONTENTS

INTRODUCTION

TO THE NEW EDITION

RE-PUBLICATION of this rare classic makes available the last major out of print book on Navajo weaving. The material was originally published as a series of small pamphlets, distributed by the Laboratory of Anthropology in Santa Fe, New Mexico[1] in the late 1930s. Subsequently, it was published in book form by the same institution in a limited edition of 1250 copies. It is almost impossible to find a copy of that limited edition today.

H. P. Mera, a keen observer with a deep interest in early material culture of the American Southwest, was an ideal person to write on the subject of Navajo textile arts and their evolution. His anthropological interests ranged broadly across the Southwest, encompassing Navajo textiles, Pueblo pottery and embroidery designs, Saltillo serapes, and Rio Grande blankets to name only a few. His special area of interest was the evolution of these early Southwest crafts and their decorative elements. In this study he focuses on style, historical evolution, and (to a lesser extent) technique in Navajo weaving.[2]

The concern and care which Mera invested in his book are especially admirable when viewed within the context of his time. The few studies in the field written before the 1930s, although of some value, were variously marred by brevity, inaccuracy, and a questionable enthusiasm for hearsay. The finest of these early works, Washington Matthews' *Navajo Weavers*, published in 1882, left many important areas unexplored. In the 1930s a great deal of important and original scholarship appeared. In 1934 Charles Avery Amsden produced *Navaho Weaving, Its*

Technic and History, a study which towered over its predecessors and has long been recognized as the definitive work in the field. Two years later Gladys Reichard's *Navajo Shepherd and Weaver* appeared, a book which detailed practical, step-by-step weaving instructions.

Then H. P. Mera, with a remarkable blend of scholarship and personal modesty, was able both to complement and to expand on without needlessly repeating these earlier writings in *Navajo Textile Arts.* His interest in styles and their evolution was one which had been only briefly discussed by others, and thus his work, with its generous use of illustrations, stands as a unique contribution.

The first edition of this book has been reproduced in its original format, a bold and simple style characteristic of Merle Armitage, the great Southwest book designer. An Afterword and an Appendix have been added in order to enhance the usefulness of the material.

Roger and Jean Moss
Berkeley, California

[1]Mention should be made here of the fact that The School of American Research (successor to The Laboratory of Anthropology) is currently developing a series of 15 volumes on Southwest Indian Art, two volumes of which will be devoted to Pueblo and Navajo weaving.

[2]Mera and other anthropologists believe that the Navajo learned weaving from the Pueblo Indians. An increasingly vocal number of traditional Navajo believe that Spider Woman inspired and directed the Navajo to weave. The present writers see Spider Woman as the guiding spirit of all weavers and believe that the skills she gave the Navajo were supplemented by technical information gleaned from their Pueblo neighbors. However, disagreements over these different ways of perceiving truth should not be allowed to overshadow the wealth of unique information on design evolution and continuity contained in this book.

A CONDENSED HISTORY
OF NAVAJO WEAVING*

UNLIKE the Pueblo Indians, whose work with textiles has been traced back some twelve hundred years, the Navajo tribe, by contrast, is known to have practised the art of weaving for little more than a mere two centuries. The first mention of woven woolen apparel in connection with the latter group occurs in a Spanish document recording observations made no earlier than the year 1706.

At this point, it is well to remember that by that time wool had practically superseded cotton, once the only fiber employed as a medium for weaving over most of the Southwest. The newer material was obtained from an Andalusian breed of sheep, imported from Spain by the way of Mexico, and not from a merino type animal, as often is stated erroneously.

It has not been made clear, however, whether the garments seen among the Navajo by the explorers of the early eighteenth century can be attributed to that people or to visiting Pueblos who are known to have fled their homes into Navajo territory to avoid reprisal for their part in the Indian rebellion of 1680-1692. Be that as it may, there can be little question that it was at this period and from these refugees that the Navajo became acquainted with the operation of the loom.

Having mastered the technique, the Navajo weavers from that time on, followed an independent line of development, one which differs in several respects from the long-established procedures of their instructors.

* A more detailed discussion of this native craft may be found in Charles Avery Amsden's "Navaho Weaving." Fine Arts Press, Santa Ana, California, 1934.

So widely-accepted was the craft and so apt were the pupils that by the last quarter of the eighteenth century, Navajo textiles had become an important article of trade in the Spanish colonies, not alone for local use but for export as well. References occurring in the scant annals of that day praise the quality of these fabrics and, at the same time, deplore the fact that the colonial weavers were able to offer little competition.

Unfortunately, no examples of blanketry are known to have survived from that period, although a few authentically dated fragments and one complete specimen illustrate the character of the weaving being done a short time later — that is, during the first years of the nineteenth century. These probably would show no particular advancement over those produced in the previous twenty-five or thirty years.

There appears to be no reason to think that any important changes in the craft took place between the beginning of the nineteenth century and the late 1840's or early 1850's. But from this time to about the middle of the 1870's, blankets marking the peak of Navajo accomplishment in loom-work appeared on the scene. This interval appropriately can be termed the "classical" period. The reason for this sudden advent of garments which exhibited both a technical excellence and a decided advance in designing may be laid to an effort to emulate the workmanship displayed in the beautifully-woven serapes of Saltillo, San Miguel, and Oaxaca in Mexico, with which the Navajo then were coming in contact. Among other considerations, such a belief is based on the considerable number of poncho-blankets (a type having a slit in the center through which the head could be passed) which were being woven at this time. Serapes possessing this poncho feature figure prominently in Mexican fashions.

It was during this "classical" period that ravelings of a red cloth, imported from England and known to the Spanish as bayeta, first were incorporated as weft elements in Navajo blanketry. This was done to obtain a brighter shade of red than was possible with any of the native dyes then available to the native artisan. Taking advantage of this break in the use of handspun yarns, certain traders succeeded in introducing three-ply yarns (Saxony and Zephyr) of European manufacture for the same purpose. Notwithstanding all of this, the average weaver continued to rely heavily on the hand-spun article for much of her work, especially for the coarser, utility types, those not intended to be used solely as a body covering.

After the mid-1870's, importation of bayeta and foreign yarns seems to have fallen off rapidly and a new chapter in the history of Navajo weaving began. Not only were the materials for the weaving of fabrics affected by altered conditions but blanketry began to take on a change in function. Bayeta, in many instances, was replaced by yarn spun from shredded and carded domestic flannels, while four-ply yarns (Germantown type) made in the United States were substituted for the earlier imported sorts. Although the use of re-spun flannel yarn is known to have lasted for only a comparatively short time, the Germantown variety continued to be employed largely until well into the 1890's. Too, the increasing ease with which White man's clothing and textiles were obtainable spelled ultimate doom for much of the hand-spun, hand-loomed garments, once deemed a necessity.

This situation might well have held a threat for the continuance of Navajo weaving, except for a happy turn of events. At the very moment that fabricated apparel of Indian manufacture appeared to be on the way out, a demand for a woven floor-covering had arisen. To supply this need, the Navajo, highly market-conscious since the very first, turned to the making of rugs. The change from weaving a textile designed for garments, susceptible of being draped, to that of a heavier and less flexible fabric was accomplished with little, if any, interruption in the activities of the craft. Since the late 1880's, Navajo weaving has been devoted almost exclusively to the production of what should more properly be termed rugs than blankets.

This broad outline is presented to serve as a background for the blanket types to be described in the following sections.

4

Plate 1
Laboratory of Anthropology $\frac{10}{466}$

Size: 49 inches by 69 inches
Colors: white and brown

1

THE SO-CALLED
"CHIEF BLANKET"

WHEN THE FIRST Spanish expeditionaries reached Pueblo territory in A.D. 1540, they were not a little surprised to find the Indians so attractively clad. It is said that their clothes were nicely woven of cotton, and ornamented with both painting and embroidery. Although we have neither detailed descriptions nor actual garments dating from this period, there is reason to believe that the same mode of dress was continued through the following centuries. And today there are forms seen on ceremonial occasions in many of the Pueblos which undoubtedly are survivals.

One of these is important to the study of textile development. It is a woman's garment planned to do duty either as a shawl, or, if wrapped around the body, as a dress. Whatever its use, the shape remains the same: an elongated rectangle, with the warp threads paralleling the short side. Today this Pueblo shawl, made from both cotton and wool, still shows patterned bands either in a woven technique or true embroidery, probably much after the general fashion noted by the early explorers.

The oblong shape with the warp following the short side seems to have been so fundamental to the structure that when the Navajo took over the art of weaving from the Pueblos it was to be expected that they would adopt a similar form. That they did this is borne out by the characteristics of some of the early Navajo blankets. However, the borrowers are believed to have woven only in wool, no cotton fabrics being recorded.

The earliest known example of Navajo weaving, illustrated in *plate 1*, was found in the grave of a mummified Navajo, and is attributed to a time fully as early as the first part of the nineteenth century. This judgment rests on two factors: the similarities in material and technique between this and the fragments recovered from the Massacre Cave dating back to 1805; and its association in the burial with two bison skins decorated in patterns produced by a heated tool. The robes in question could not have been of a much later period, because the tooling method was being replaced by painted designs at about the turn of the century. The entire scheme of decoration in this primitive piece of Navajo weaving consists in the alternation of longitudinal brown stripes with white ones.

To such simple beginnings may be traced the later, more complex, design on what is known commercially as the "chief blanket." The name "chief blanket" is a misnomer, as this blanket was never intended to designate the rank of the wearer. Although the term appears to be of commercial origin, it has been incorporated in the literature on Navajo weaving to cover a definitely-recognized design sequence which is described here. Two distinct types are commonly included under this heading: one of comparatively small size, with a background of many narrow stripes; the other much larger, in which the stripes are typically broad and few. The first was planned for women, since, while it was large enough to protect the shoulders, it would at the same time leave arms and legs free for household tasks.

The larger blankets, big enough to wrap the whole body, apparently were thought better suited to men. These two forms remained distinct until some time after the introduction of White man's clothing, which ultimately turned the weaving industry from the making of garments to the manufacture of rugs.

With either type, the first departure from the simple arrangement of alternating brown and white stripes of nearly uniform width appears to have been the very considerable widening of the two marginal brown stripes. Within the broad borders thus formed were inserted narrow lengthwise stripes of blue. Presumably the blue dye used for this purpose was obtained by trade from Mexico, where indigo-producing plants are native, although there is a possibility that commercial indigo may have been imported by then.

About this time the weavers began to divide the striped field lengthwise with another wide band. This normally included narrow blue stripes to match those on the margin. The stripe was essentially made up of two of the marginal bands placed side by side *(plate 2)*.

The next innovation was the insertion of oblong blocks of red in the center and ends of both the median and lateral bands *(plate 3)*. The first material employed for this color consisted almost exclusively of strands raveled from a cloth called, by the Spanish merchants, *bayeta*. This was a standard item of trade for many years in the Southwest, and appears to have been in great demand, probably because there were no native red dyes of so lively a shade. A widely-current story that

Plate 2
Laboratory of Anthropology; Stewart Collection $\frac{10}{2222}$
Size: 56 inches by 71 inches
Colors: white, blue, and black

Plate 3
Laboratory of Anthropology; gift of Miss A. E. White

$\frac{10}{2175}$

8

Size: 54 inches by 72 inches
Colors: white, brown, blue, and red

Plate 4
Laboratory of Anthropology; Stewart Collection $\frac{10}{438}$

Size: 55 inches by 75 inches
Colors: white, brown-black, blue, and red

this color was made from soldiers' raveled uniforms has not the slightest foundation in fact.

From this point, further developments of blanket design may be said, curiously enough, to be influenced by the sex of the wearer. In the case of the smaller or woman's blanket, the three wider bands, two marginal and one median, running the entire length of the blanket continue to hold the central place in the decorative scheme. In the larger man's blanket these become secondary to the elaboration of the end and center blocks. Besides these differences, the woman's garment maintains much narrower background stripes, which often are woven of a light grey where white would be normal for the larger sizes *(plates 7, 8, 9 and 10)*.

In the man's blanket, following the small solid oblong insertions, larger open quadrangular figures appear *(plate 4)*. These, in turn, eventually were replaced by stepped diagonals running across the corners and on all

Plate 5
Laboratory of Anthropology; Stewart Collection $\frac{10}{413}$
Size: 55 inches by 71 inches
Colors: white, black, blue, red, and yellow

four margins to form triangles, while those in the center of the blanket were arranged to outline diamond- or lozenge-shaped areas *(plate 5)*. These enclosed spaces were utilized for a great variety of decorative treatments.

The late "chief blankets," perhaps more properly called "rugs," are apt to show an increased complexity of design, especially after the introduction of Germantown yarns. The central diamond-shaped unit and the angular units at the corners and on the margins assumed a growing importance, and often were expanded to such an extent that the striped backgrounds, though always present, became only a minor interest *(plate 6)*. Notwithstanding the many alterations in pattern, the fundamental arrangement of a warp which followed the direction of the least width was maintained throughout all evolutionary changes.

In spite of continued elaboration, it must not be thought that the more elemental forms were completely discarded. Examples may be found woven of a material which places the piece at a far later period than the design alone would justify.

A number of materials may be used in helping to estimate the period of manufacture. Excluding handspun yarns, which were used at all periods, they follow, in broadly chronological sequence: ravelings from a fine textured imported cloth, used in two or more strands; ravelings of a much coarser fabric, used in one strand; imported three-ply Saxony and Zephyr yarns; domestic flannels raveled, carded and respun; and commercial four-ply yarns, usually lumped under the term Germantown. The type of dye is also of use in the determination of the age of a blanket, since the use of cochineal and vegetal dyes preceded that of aniline or other commercial varieties, except recently, where the former have been re-introduced.

All of the above factors, rather than any single criterion, must be considered before judging the age of an undated specimen.

Plate 6
Loan: H. H. Kramer (Lab. of Anth. reg. No. 341)

Size: 46 inches by 70 inches

Colors: white, black, blue-green, pink, red, and maroon   **11**

Plate 7
Indian Arts Fund T 370

Size: 37 inches by 54 inches

Colors: grey, black, dark blue, red, and green

Plate 8

Indian Arts Fund T 4

Size: 46 inches by 62 inches

Colors: grey, brown, blue, scarlet, green, and black

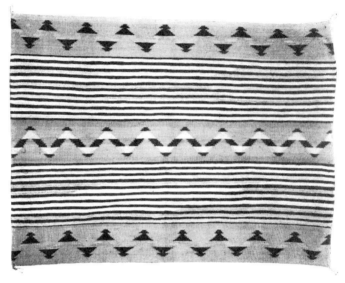

Plate 9

Indian Arts Fund T 362

Size: 39 inches by 50 inches

Colors: grey, black, blue, red, pale green, and dull yellow

Plate 10
Indian Arts Fund T 361

Size: 52 inches by 56 inches

Colors: grey, black, deep blue, red, white, and dark green   **13**

2 🐐

NAVAJO BLANKETS OF
THE "CLASSIC" PERIOD

WEAVING, the supreme craft of Navajo women, has held its own for a great many years as one of the most important products of the Indian Southwest. Meager references to the art in early Spanish documents show that shortly before the year 1800 it had begun to receive a degree of recognition. Of the output of those early times, however, only one complete specimen and a few odd fragments have survived.

Following these early examples, others apparently are unknown until the middle of the century, but by that time it is quite evident that in the interim both quality of design and technique of weaving had attained a high degree of excellence. During a period beginning with the early 1850's and continuing into the 1870's blankets were woven which represent the highest expression of the weaver's skill. It is to this era of excellence that the term "classic" is here applied. However, it must not be thought that all blanketry produced within this period was outstanding, as a number of early photographs show that the simply-striped, coarse-textured blanket still was in use for ordinary wear.

"Classic" blankets, for convenience, may be divided broadly into two groups: one, in which the background is composed of narrow stripes *(plate 11)*; the other, in which these features are lacking *(plate 12)* or are largely subordinated *(plate 13)*. There are many intergradations between the two, as the designs on both always include at least some form of the stripe, either simple, interrupted, or in the guise of derivatives.

It appears to be a reasonable deduction that, some-

Plate 11

Laboratory of Anthropology; Yontz Collection $\frac{10}{367}$
Poncho type. Size: 53 inches by 82 inches
Colors: white, blue, green, and red (raveled material)

Plate 12

Loan: Nathan B. Stern (Lab. of Anth. reg. No. 124)
Size: 53 inches by 73 inches
Colors: white, blue, mulberry (raveled material),
and madder (raveled material)

Plate 13

Laboratory of Anthropology; Stewart Collection $\frac{10}{432}$

Size: 53 inches by 73 inches

Colors: white (Saxony), blue, madder (Saxony), and green (raveled material)

Plate 14

Laboratory of Anthropology $\frac{10}{407}$

Size: 54 inches by 72 inches

Colors: white, blue, and red (raveled material)

time between the first and middle parts of the nineteenth century, weavers, in an attempt to get away from the severity and monotony of simple stripes, began to convert these into zigzags. The diagonals required in producing these zigzags, on account of limitations imposed by the art of weaving, had to be produced by means of a series of steps, which gives a somewhat terraced outline *(plate 14)*. At times a number of these zigzag stripes were joined at top and bottom to form reticulated patterns which often are found superimposed on narrowly-striped backgrounds *(plates 11 and 15)*. In other instances, bands composed of zigzags appear on plain backgrounds, interspersed with detached figures based on the principle of the terrace *(plate 14)*. Forms derived from sections of the zigzag were used also to outline angular or lozenge-shaped spaces. These were located at the corners, sides, and centers of blankets, the enclosed areas being filled in with smaller design units *(plates 14 and 17)*. Similar figures occu-

Plate 15

Laboratory of Anthropology; Stewart Collection $\frac{10}{1947}$

Poncho type. Size: 55 inches by 83 inches

Colors: white, blue, and red (raveled material)

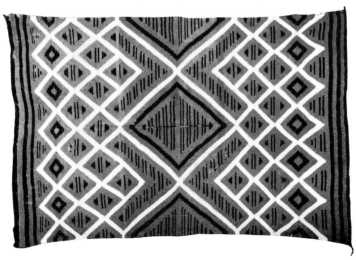

pying identical situations on so-called "chief" blankets undoubtedly were derived from this source.

On fine blankets of this period, no matter how intricate the patterns may appear at first sight, an analysis of the typical designs, without reference to the character of background, will show that all merely consist of ingenious arrangements based on two fundamental forms: simple stripes and stepped zigzags or portions thereof. This appearance of complexity is, of course, greatly aided by the different colors used to produce contrasts in the several repeating parts of compounded design structures.

It was during the classical period that raveled strands of bayeta, a trade-cloth, usually red in color, were utilized extensively in weaving. Less frequently employed were imported three-ply yarns which resemble the modern materials now called Saxony and Zephyr. In order to match the small size and the even machine-spinning

Plate 16

Indian Arts Fund (gift of Miss A. E. White) T 175

Size: 58 inches by 81 inches

Colors: white, blue, pink, and olive green (all yarn used in this blanket is Zephyr)

of these commercial yarns, the Indian craftsman was forced to fabricate a yarn of a quality never since equalled in the history of Navajo weaving.

A matter worthy of more than passing interest lies in the fact that many "classic" blankets were woven with a slit in their centers large enough to admit the head, thus converting them into ponchos *(plates 11 and 15)*. As this treatment is a very unusual proceeding for known aboriginal blanketry north of Mexico, it appears to be well within the limits of possibility that these fine examples represent attempts to emulate in quality, if not in design, those exquisitely-woven serapes and ponchos produced in the Saltillo and San Miguel districts of Mexico.

In the years following the "classic period," progressively fewer fine examples were woven. The whole

Plate 17

Laboratory of Anthropology; Stewart Collection $\frac{10}{447}$

Size: 54 inches by 74 inches

Colors: white, blue, rose (raveled material), and green (raveled material)

trend was toward thicker and coarser textures. This in a great measure was due to an increasing demand for articles suitable for use as floor coverings. Fine weaving comparable to that of the "classic" type became practically extinct until the later advent of four-ply commercial (Germantown) yarns made it almost impossible to produce other than even, closely-woven rugs. Although, in a purely technical way, weaving (which utilized this machine-spun yarn) yielded products of a more even texture than did those in which hand-spun yarn was used, designs of the later periods definitely lack the classic dignity so characteristic of the earlier type of textile.

3

THE "SLAVE BLANKET"

THE TERM "slave blanket" is used to designate a class of Southwestern blanketry in which there is a curious blending of Navajo upright loom technique and design with dyes and minor decorative motifs typical of those used by the Spanish colonists.

A clue to the reason for such a mixture of styles is to be found in records dealing with the mode of life in the colonies. In these accounts numerous references to Apache slaves may be found, among which some are distinguished as Apaches de Navahu, or, in later parlance, Navajos. Mention also is made of frequent raids between Spanish and Navajo. Such forays appear to have been undertaken by the Indians for the acquisition of livestock, and by the Spanish for obtaining slaves. Expeditions of this nature are known to have been carried on by both sides as late as the 1860's.

Among the Indian captives thus taken, often there were women skilled in weaving. These, according to reliable tradition, were put to work producing textiles for the family or community to which they were apportioned.

It was quite natural that these weavers should prefer their own upright loom, and for this reason they were permitted to continue the use of a method with which they were most familiar. Although unhampered in regard to the choice of loom, they were apparently denied ready access to their own dyes, and therefore were forced to rely upon those in use by their captors. In addition to being obliged to use strange coloring-matters, these women were subjected to another influence which was to alter, to a limited extent, their ideas on decoration. This influence was contact with Mexican

Plate 18
Indian Arts Fund T 342

Size: 53 inches by 76 inches
Colors: tan, blue green, orange, red, and lavender

Plate 19
Indian Arts Fund (gift of Miss A. E. White) T 189
Size: 49 inches by 81 inches
Colors: white, black, blue, and red (raveled material)

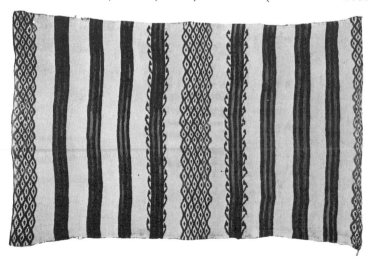

designs, which could be seen on serapes imported from the South by the Spanish colonists. It is not at all surprising that in the patterns appearing on blankets woven by Navajo slaves, certain features taken from Mexican sources may be found incorporated, although these textiles otherwise are basically Navajoan in concept. One of the most evident of these derivations occurring in occasional slave blankets is a centrally-placed, diamond-shaped area of decoration which in Mexican serapes is the principal feature *(compare plates 23 and 24 with plate 25)*.

Because of the dyes employed, simply-designed "slave blankets," especially the plain, striped type *(plate 18)*, at first sight may pass as the work of Spanish artisans. However, those on which a greater degree of elaboration of design appears are not so easily mistaken.

Of even greater value in the matter of identification are certain details of technique which may be relied upon to furnish proof of their origin upon the Navajo or upright type of loom. Two of the more obvious are a braided selvage on all edges and the occurrence of "lazy lines." As regards the first of these, it can be stated that the writer has not yet found in any of the numerous specimens examined an example of harness-loom weaving that possesses this feature.

"Lazy line" is a name applied to those diagonal markings that appear to break the continuity of an otherwise evenly-woven surface. These are caused by a purposeful failure to carry certain weft elements entirely across the web formed by the warp threads. That is, a weft element is woven back and forth from one edge towards the center, progressively receding a distance of one or more warps as the work proceeds. After reaching the desired height, the weaver moves to the opposite side and repeats the performance from that edge. As a consequence, where the two sections join, a diagonal line of interruptions occur. A procedure of this nature is little short of impossible on a harness-loom.

Plate 20
Indian Arts Fund T 21

Size: 51 inches by 82 inches
Colors: mottled pink, purple, madder,
vermilion, and orange

Plate 21
Laboratory of Anthropology $\frac{10}{399}$

Size: 45 inches by 66 inches
Colors: white, brown, madder, pale green, and apricot

Less constant as a factor for determining blankets in the "slave" class is the type of warp used, as both single and two-ply kinds were employed. The former was, and is, the standard usage for Navajo textiles but the latter is identified so definitely with Mexican weaving that when it is found in blankets demonstrating upright loom work, such examples may be suspected at once of being the work of some captive weaver.

Although no dated specimens are known, it is evident that a majority of recorded "slave blankets," judged by the character of their designs, were produced at a time when the Navajo "classic blanket" still was in fashion; or perhaps patterns of the classic period were the only style remembered by the weavers *(plates 21 and 22)*. Again, examples are known in which strands of raveled cloth were incorporated, a practise largely discontinued in Indian weaving soon after the close of

Plate 22
Indian Arts Fund T 343

Size: 57 inches by 75½ inches
Colors: white, blue, light green, orange, cerise, pomegranate, magenta, lavender, violet, and purple

the "classic" period in the early 1870's. All this suggests that a great many blankets of this type were woven about the middle of the nineteenth century.

The practise of enslaving Indians in New Mexico lessened, and finally ceased altogether, largely because of the activities of Archbishop Lamy during his term of office (1851-1888).

From the foregoing it will be seen that a number of criteria must be used to determine the authenticity of "slave blankets." These are: loom technique, design, dyes, and, to a lesser extent, the type of warp.

Plate 23
Indian Arts Fund T 333

Size: 49 inches by 85 inches
Colors: white, vermilion, orange, lavender,
green, blue, brown, and grey

Plate 24
Laboratory of Anthropology; Harry Kelly Collection $\frac{10}{477}$
Poncho type. Size: 50 inches by 86 inches
Colors: white, brown, blue, and red (raveled material)   **27**

Plate 25
Laboratory of Anthropology (gift of M. J. Van Houten)
$\frac{10}{2144}$
Mexican serape. Size: 52 inches by 90 inches
Colors: white, blue, tan, yellow, pink,
madder, and light blue

4 🐐

PICTORIAL BLANKETS

28 PURELY geometric designs are so typical of Navajo blanketry that it becomes a matter of some surprise to many to learn that there are a number of blankets in existence on which graphic representations have been included in the decorative scheme. Houses, railroad trains, and a variety of life-forms were utilized at times for such purposes. In the latter category are to be found representations of human figures, horses, cattle, birds, and, more rarely, some of the invertebrates, such as insects *(plate 27)*.

The earliest blanket known to the writer on which

Plate 26
Indian Arts Fund T 43

Size: 56 inches by 76 inches
Colors: white, lavender, orchid, light blue, yellow, light and dark red, black, dark blue, peach, tan, light and dark green, and pink. (Marginal arrows indicate small bird forms)

life-forms appear is one taken from the body of an Indian killed during the Sand Creek massacre of 1864 *(plate 26)*. In this instance four small, inconspicuous bird-figures resembling ducks were located near the four corners of a median band of design, although in all other respects decorative details were of the "classic" type.

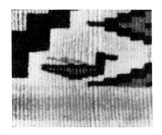

Detail 1
Bird figure from plate 26

Most pictorial blankets, however, are believed to post-date that early example at least by some fifteen to

Plate 27

Loan: Wheaton Augur (Lab. of Anth. registered No. 109)
Size:
　55½ inches by
　72 inches
Colors:
　white,
　buff,
　orange,
　henna,
　vermilion,
　green,
　brown,
　grey,
　and
　tan

Plate 28

30

Loan: Wheaton
Augur (Lab. of
Anth. registered
No. 108)
Size:
    58 inches by
    69 inches
Colors:
    white,
    grey,
    vermilion,
    black,
    and
    yellow

Plate 29

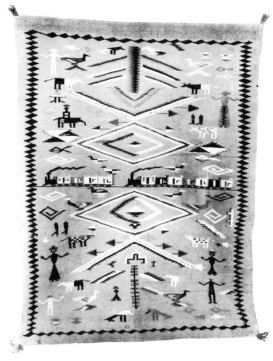

Laboratory of
Anthropology;
Stewart Collection
    $\frac{10}{1946}$
Size:
    61 inches by
    80 inches
Colors:
    white,
    black,
    blue,
    green,
    yellow,
    lavender,
    and
    red

twenty years. This judgment is based on the materials employed and the generally thick and heavy character of the weave. Using these same two criteria, it would appear that the greater number were produced during a time when four-ply commercial yarns, usually lumped under the term Germantown, were largely in use by Navajo weavers. This period would fall roughly between the late 1870's and the early years of the twentieth century. A blanket in which some four-ply yarn was used and which was secured at Fort Wingate circa 1880, will illustrate a typical example of that period *(plate 28)*.

Although the limitations of loom technique imposed a very definite handicap, it is plainly to be seen that in most cases the weaver has made every effort to depict objects as naturalistically as possible. On the other hand, there are others which indicate that the maker approached her problem in a highly whimsical mood *(plate 29)*.

In an effort to achieve satisfactory representations of natural subjects, ingenious deviations from the normal procedure of weaving sometimes were called into play. Thus, when dealing with the slant necessary to represent an animal's tail, a few strands of weft element of the proper length, and held in place by a little yarn of the ground color, were woven diagonally to the axis of the warp. Following this, weaving proceeded horizontally in the usual manner on both sides of the diagonal section thus formed *(plate 30)*. This was done in order to avoid what normally would appear as a stepped line.

Quite a number of blankets, particularly some of those portraying horses and cattle, were executed with the figures woven in black or some other somber color on a white ground. This variety in some parts of the Southwest popularly is called a "burial blanket" *(plates 31 and 32)*. It is difficult to determine how such an idea has come to be associated with blankets of this type. It may be that it relates to the well-known Navajo cus-

Plate 30

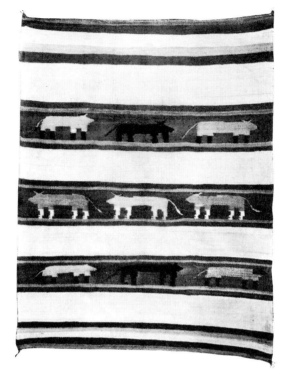

Indian Arts Fund
T 9
Size:
   52 inches by
   69 inches
Colors:
   white,
   vermilion,
   black,
   pale green,
   yellow-green,
   and
   deep yellow

Plate 31

Indian Arts Fund
T 405
Size:
   60 inches by
   83 inches
Colors:
   white and
   brown

tom of sacrificing a horse at the grave of its owner. On the other hand, the term may, perhaps, have come into use through our own association of black and white with mourning. At all events, since no authentic record exists concerning the weaving of a special type of blanket for funereal purposes, the term "burial blanket" in all probability is quite fictitious.

In fact, none of the realistic features on pictorial blankets has an appearance of being derived from anything of a ceremonial or ritualistic nature, including sandpaintings, which might appear to have been a likely source. For this reason, those products of current Navajo weaving known commercially as "yeibichai rugs" *(plate 33)* in no way should be confused with the earlier class of textile which forms the subject of this section. As far as can be determined, the later style cannot be

Plate 32

Laboratory of
Anthropology
$\frac{10}{3307}$
Size:
45 inches by
64 inches
Colors:
white,
brown,
and
orange

Plate 33

Indian Arts Fund
(gift of Miss
A. E. White)
T 114
Size:
  51 inches by
  52 inches
Colors:
  white,
  brown,
  black,
  red,
  green,
  yellow,
  and
  purple

Plate 34
Laboratory of Anthropology; Stewart Collection $\frac{10}{448}$
Size: 88 inches by 98 inches
Colors: grey, black, white, red, blue, brown, and orange

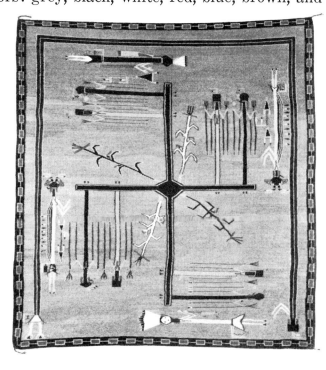

viewed as a direct development out of any earlier fashion, and must be considered as something entirely new.

Another, less familiar, type of rug in the pictorial class *(plate 34)*, bears replicas of actual sandpaintings. A few rugs of this sort have been woven in the face of strong Navajo disapproval. It will be found, however, that in most examples some essential detail has been represented incorrectly, probably in the hope that retribution might be averted for an overt act of sacrilege.

5 🐃

BANDED-BACKGROUND

BLANKETS

36 THERE IS a very distinctive style of Indian blanket which Amsden has described by the term, "Moqui pattern." This is derived from an obsolete name that once was applied to the Hopi people. Because of the derivation, people inadvertently may get the impression that the term is connected solely with Hopi weaving. Actually, the great majority of such blankets are of Navajo origin, and only a comparatively few of the type can be ascribed with any certainty to other weavers. For these reasons it has seemed wise to propose the designation, "banded-background blankets," as a more descriptive term.

As the proposed name indicates, the distinctive feature of these blankets is a background consisting of narrow bands woven transversely to the direction of the warp. There is little doubt that this style originally was of Pueblo origin, since Navajo weaving admittedly is derived from Puebloan sources. Judging from the few surviving samples of early nineteenth century Navajo blanketry, decorative features in the beginning appear to have followed a basic treatment of crosswise stripes of varying widths. Even as late as the "classic" period of Navajo weaving (circa 1850-1875), when a large degree of elaboration was coming into vogue, all designs still were based on the stripe or some of its modifications. Despite the fact that the general movement always was toward greater and greater complexity of design, the Navajo never has entirely discarded the simply-striped form.

If one may judge from authenticated specimens, it seems safe to say that while the Navajo experimented with increasingly elaborate designs, the Pueblo never strayed far from original patterns. The extreme conservatism of the Pueblo weavers caused them to remain, largely, content with the early fashion of plain striping, and they developed few innovations of any value in identifying a distinctively Pueblo style. It thus becomes practically impossible to distinguish a simply-striped blanket of Navajo weaving from one of Pueblo manufacture.

Many dealers, confronted with this situation, are likely to classify nearly all of the simply-striped blankets as Hopi. Probably they choose this as the easiest way out. But this classification brings up a further complication, because exactly this same type of blanket also was woven in the villages of Zuni and Acoma until a few years ago. For these reasons, it seems evident that the term Pueblo should be preferred over that of Hopi when referring to blankets believed to be of Puebloan manufacture, unless the actual village in which they were woven is known.

Another error frequently made in commercial circles is to class as Hopi blankets very obviously of Navajo origin. The blankets show the banded background and for that reason the dealer tosses them into his catch-all Hopi classification. This is done in spite of the fact that such blankets have, in addition to the banded background, more elaborate designs that show strongly-marked Navajo characteristics.

Navajo blankets in the banded-background category can be distinguished from all other classes by a field almost entirely composed of narrow alternating bands of black or brown and blue. This treatment was inherited from the past. Later, during a revival of the style, when commercial four-ply (Germantown) yarns were largely employed, a purple or purplish-blue shade was substituted for the earlier indigo. This apparently was due to the failure of the aniline dyes then in use to furnish a better match. Such a combination of colors naturally resulted in giving the whole a somber cast. Usually the only relief was supplied by other narrow stripes of white

Plate 35
Laboratory of Anthropology (gift of Mrs. J. W. Chapman)
$\frac{10}{2475}$
Size: 51 inches by 68 inches
Colors: white, black, and blue

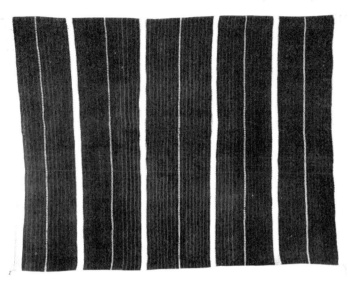

Plate 36
Laboratory of Anthropology $\frac{10}{406}$
Size: 50 inches by 72 inches
Colors: white, blue, black, red, pink, yellow, and green

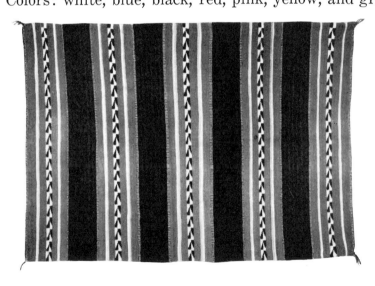

or some contrasting color, few in number and widely-spaced *(plate 35)*.

If the Navajo weavers intended a blanket to remain strictly in the Pueblo tradition, no ornamentation was attempted beyond simple striping. Usually, however, the Navajo's liking for bright colors prevailed. A variety of colorful patterns was added in such a manner that they give the impression of being superimposed on the banded background.

There was a great diversity of design thus employed. These designs range from broad bands of some lively color, which often include a series of decorative devices *(plate 36)*, to the terraced designs of the "classic" era *(plates 37 and 38)*, and on to later styles in which serrations were a principal feature *(plate 39)*. On this basis it is possible, in certain cases, to form some judgment concerning the period in which a blanket was woven.

Plate 37
Indian Arts Fund (gift of Miss A. E. White) T 103
Size: 50 inches by 70 inches
Colors: white, blue, black, and pink

Plate 38

Laboratory of Anthropology; Stewart Collection $\frac{10}{430}$

Size: 52 inches by 72 inches

40

Colors: white, blue, black, vermilion (respun flannel), green, and blue-green (Germantown)

Plate 39

Laboratory of Anthropology (gift of James F. Simon) $\frac{10}{2185}$

Size: 50 inches by 66 inches

Colors: brown, blue, green, and pink

In other instances the materials used in weaving, such as raveled cloth, shredded and respun flannel, or Saxony yarn, also help to furnish a clue as to age.

From a survey of weaving materials and designs, it is safe to state that the banded-background style persisted from at least the early 1870's well into the 1880's. Later, a revival of the type *(plate 40)* based on "classic" designs but woven from commercial four-ply yarns took place, principally at Hubbell's Trading Post, Ganado, Arizona. During this renaissance large numbers were produced, thus extending the life of the banded-background style through the 1890's. These later examples, however, were intended for use as rugs. In this respect they differ from the earlier kinds, which were utilized principally as outer garments.

Plate 40
Laboratory of Anthropology $\frac{10}{492}$
Size: 62 inches by 75 inches
Colors: white, black, red, and purple (all Germantown)

6

WEDGE-WEAVE BLANKETS

THE TERM "wedge-weave" has been adopted for a very interesting and little noticed technique in Navajo blanketry. It is a variant from the usual course of tapestry weaving among the Navajo.

Wedge-weave blankets have a characteristic zigzag pattern. Their sides are never even, but are wavy or scalloped in outline *(plate 42)*. The reason for the uneven sides lies in the fact that the particular technique employed necessarily distorts the warp.

The procedure for making a blanket of this type, following a variable number of rows of normal tapestry weave as a base, calls for the weaving of a wedge-like

Plate 41
Indian Arts Fund
(Gift of Miss Mary C. Wheelwright) T 56
                          Size: 51 inches by 68 inches
Colors: white, black, pink, orange, green, and yellow-green

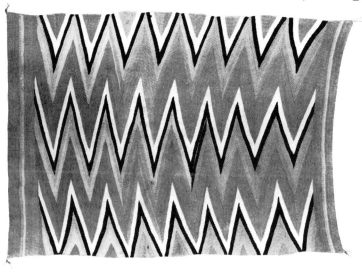

section, in the form of a right-angle triangle, in what is to be one of the lower corners. The hypotenuse of the triangle lies obliquely to the normal direction of the warp and slants toward the center, while the other two sides of this section follow the bottom and one side of the proposed fabric.

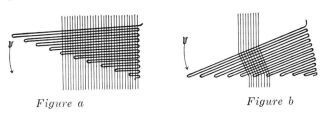

Figure a   Figure b

In order to accomplish the slope required by this preliminary wedge, weaving is started by first including only a few of the warp threads, and as the work continues upward, by gradually using more and more of them *(figure a)*. Meanwhile, care is taken to keep the weft packed down to the required angle. By this method

Plate 42
Indian Arts Fund (gift of Henry G. Stevens) T 47
Size: 73 inches by 75 inches
Colors: white, brown, grey, red, and orange

of battening, the warp is distorted from the perpendicular and passes through the weft at almost right angles to the upper edge of this wedge-shaped section *(figure b)*.

After the needed slope is established, a number of oblique stripes in contrasting colors are added. These follow the angle set by the hypotenuse of the first wedge and are woven up to a predetermined and uniform height. Both the upper and lower ends of these stripes are woven in such a way that the end meets the horizontal in an acute angle *(figure c)*.

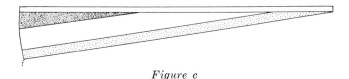

Figure c

A whole series of these stripes is carried entirely across the work. When weaving reaches the other side of the loom, however, the final figure produced is not a stripe but another triangle: like the first, but inverted *(figure d)*. At this point the fabric presents the appearance of a band composed of diagonal stripes, with triangles filling out opposite corners. Crossing these stripes may be traced the warp threads running at right angles to the weft *(figure e)*.

Figure d

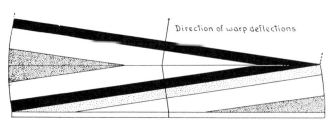

Direction of warp deflections

Figure e

The next step is to follow in the reverse direction the procedure just described. Thus, the beginning wedge of the next band is on the opposite side of the loom from the initial wedge of the first band, directly above its triangular vestige of stripe. In the second band the stripes slant in the opposite direction from those below *(figure e)*. Since these opposing stripes meet at an acute angle to form a series like a repetition of the letter V, extending from one side of the blanket to the other, the widths of the stripes usually are carefully matched. In many cases the entire blanket is composed of these bands which together form an all-over zigzag pattern *(plates 41 and 42)*. At other times wedge-weave bands are alternated with others of the usual simple tapestry weaving *(plates 43 and 44)*. The majority of wedge-weave blankets are inclined to be coarse in texture. Comparatively few examples may be considered at all finely woven.

Hand-spun yarns, dyed with aniline colors, appear to have been used most frequently, but examples woven of

Plate 43
Indian Arts Fund T 6

Size: 50 inches by 75 inches
Colors: white, black, vermilion, scarlet, and orange

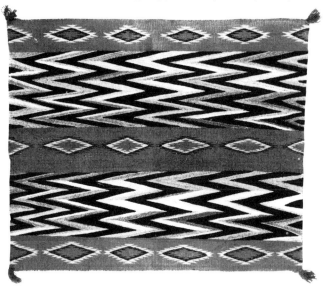

Plate 44
Laboratory of Anthropology; Stewart Collection $\frac{10}{416}$
Size: 42 inches by 50 inches
Colors: grey, black, blue, red, and green

Plate 45
Indian Arts Fund T 367

Size: 49 inches by 75 inches
Colors: white, black, rust brown, tan, grey,
yellow, salmon, orange, vermilion, and red

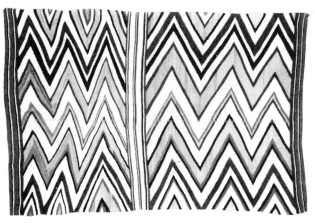

the four-ply commercial kinds occasionally are found. The latter class includes those of finest weave. This is due to the fine, even character of machine-spun yarn and to the fact that any hand-spun yarn used to fill out has to be scaled to a similar size to secure uniform appearance.

Why a technique of this kind should have been developed remains problematical, since the care and time involved appears to have been somewhat greater than in ordinary tapestry weaving. On first thought, it might be reasoned that the zigzag effect thus achieved was superior to that arrived at by the usual minutely stepped method *(figure f)*.

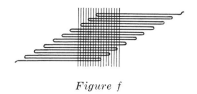

Figure f

This, however, does not seem to hold, as may be seen by the example in *plate 45*. The part of this blanket lying below the dividing band is wedge-weave; that above is ordinary tapestry weave. It is at once evident that the zigzags of the upper portion present an appearance as good, if not better, than those of the lower section, even without considering the distortion of the edges resulting from use of the wedge-weave technique.

Whatever the reason, this peculiar fashion enjoyed considerable popularity over a period beginning somewhere in the 1880's *(plate 44)* and extending into the 1890's. The style is not known to have survived this era and does not seem to have been revived in more recent times.

7

THE SERRATE DESIGNS
OF NAVAJO BLANKETRY

48 FOLLOWING the elementally stepped and terraced designs characteristic of the "classic" period, there developed, progressively, a move to get away from forms which had been almost entirely based on the rectangular. This was a natural impulse, as history records that there is ever a tendency in any simple art to strive for greater degrees of elaboration. One of the most noticeable alterations was accomplished by the substitution of acute-angles for right-angles. When this was done, ordinary steps became transformed into a series of serrations, as illustrated.

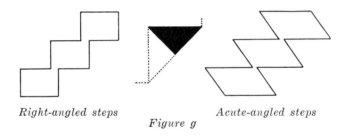

Right-angled steps   *Acute-angled steps*

Figure g

The new serrate style, based on the use of acutely angled elements, rapidly reached a high degree of popularity, and by the late 1870's had, to a large extent, succeeded in replacing the older, simply-stepped patterns.

This transition between the old and the new took place about the time aniline dyes were making their appearance at the traders' stores and, in consequence, a great majority of blankets bearing serrate designs show the use of this kind of dye. Nevertheless, a few may be seen in which ravelings from cloth (bayeta) or, at times, a three-ply commercial yarn (commonly known as Saxony) were employed — materials usually associated with the blanketry of the previous period.

About the time that three-ply yarns and those obtained by raveling cloth were passing from the picture, a new material came into existence. This was obtained from common red flannel which (because it could not be successfully raveled in strands sufficiently long for weaving) laboriously had to be picked to pieces, carded, and then respun. Yarn of this type also may be met with in textiles having serrate designs.

Though four-ply commercial yarns (Germantown) were beginning to be utilized toward the end of the 1870's, it will be noted that, in the earlier examples in particular, the use of hand-spun exceeded that of all others. Later, the situation at various times became practically reversed, especially in the late 1880's and the succeeding decade.

The simplest application of the serrate principle was to use it as a substitute for the zigzag line or band of

Plate 46
Indian Arts Fund (gift of H. P. Mera) T 317
Size: 52 inches by 76 inches
Colors: white, vermilion, pink, carded grey, brown-black

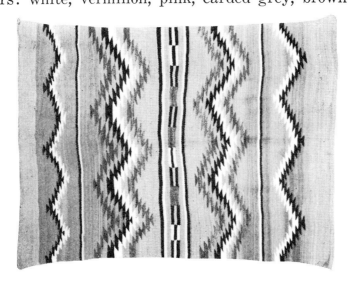

stepped elements which was such a prominent feature in the "classic" period. An example of this usage is shown in *plate 46*. A slightly greater degree of elaboration for blanket patterns could be obtained by interspersing detached lozenge-shaped design units in the spaces between these zigzags *(plate 47)*. Reticulated effects were produced from diagonally-placed rows of serrations by dividing the field into angular sections *(plate 48)*.

Quite a different-shaped unit was obtained when two series of these elements were placed back to back and woven in a single color. In such an event, a line of more or less diamond-shaped figures is seen to have resulted *(plate 49)*. Such figures in short series, or completely detached, were used in many different ways, often as constituent parts in combination with other distinctive styles.

At other times, the angles of serrations were reduced to such an extreme that a fringe-like effect was achieved

Plate 47
Laboratory of Anthropology (gift of Miss M. V. Conkey)

$\frac{10}{1940}$

Size: 53 inches by 77 inches
Colors: white, indigo blue, red, yellow, green, and olive green

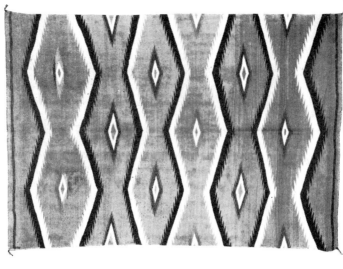

Plate 48
Indian Arts Fund (gift of H. P. Mera) T 324
Size: 55½ inches by 83 inches
Colors: white, carded light grey, red and
dark red, carded dark grey

Plate 49
Indian Arts Fund (gift of H. P. Mera) T 325
Size: 60 inches by 71 inches
Colors: white, black, carded grey

Plate 50
Laboratory of Anthropology (gift of Mrs. E. B. Dane)

$\frac{10}{2523}$

Size: 49 inches by 75 inches

Colors: white, indigo blue, grey (Saxony), green (Saxony), yellow (Saxony), red (raveled material)

Plate 51
Laboratory of Anthropology; Stewart Collection $\frac{10}{436}$

Size: 31 inches by 37 inches

Colors: white, black, henna, scarlet, grey, green, yellow, yellow-green, light brown, faded purple, blue grey (all Germantown)

(plate 50). There are other variations, too numerous to be included here, based on this principle, all of which are easily traceable to that same source.

In all probability, what may be regarded as the highest degree of complexity was obtained from the use of a number of parallel series of serrate elements which were so arranged that a solid mass composed of triangular figures and rhombs was formed *(plate 51)*.

From the inception of the serrate idea there has been no break in the continuity of its usage, in some form or other, up to the present day. In fact, it may be said that the style, including its derivatives, has become as readily recognizable as a part of Navajo weaving as is the simple upright loom, on which the textiles displaying such designs are woven.

Because of the great variety of applications to which serrations are put and the many combinations with other and more strongly-marked styles in which they play only a minor role, it has been impossible to create any single class for all blankets demonstrating this type of design.

8 🐐

THE ZONING TREATMENT IN NAVAJO BLANKET DESIGN

54 THE TERM "zoning" has been selected to describe the manner of dividing the fields of blankets into sections by means of decorative bands woven horizontally to the direction of the warp. Arrangements of this sort manifestly require a minimum of skill to produce and constituted, probably, the earliest form of decorative device employed, save perhaps for that used on the banded-background type.

In its most elemental form a zoned blanket, as far as the technique of weaving goes, is related very closely to the simplest form of the banded-background sort, the only difference being in the arrangement and number of stripes. The latter fashion employs these to cover the entire surface of a fabric; while in the other, such features are gathered into groups, which appear as zones on a plain field.

Although the idea apparently originated as regularly-spaced groups of stripes intended to relieve the monotony of an otherwise plain expanse, the division of a blanket into alternating wide bands or zones of decoration, with others left undecorated, became accepted in the course of time as one of a number of fixed and standard formulas of design.

There can be but little doubt that, after the simplest stage had become well established, it was discovered that a zone could be made much more pleasing by varying widths of the several stripes of which it was composed, or by having those stripes appear on a band of color differing from that of the undecorated intervals.

Still another way was discovered to modify the appearance of a stripe. This was accomplished by a method of weaving called "beading," which gave the stripes the appearance of horizontal rows of small blocks of alternating colors.

Later on, it was only natural that when Navajo textile design had developed in both variety and complexity, many of the newer decorative effects were used to elaborate, and even to supplant, the more elemental striped zone. Although a great many such changes eventually took place, the earlier established basic divisions of the field into decorated and plain sections continued, little altered.

So numerous are the types of design that have been used in zoned blankets that only a few can be listed here. *Plate 52* illustrates the simplest form, wherein multiple stripes compose the zone of decoration; and in *plate 53* the variation called "beading" is shown.

During the classical period, stepped and terraced designs were included in the bands *(plate 54)*. Following

Plate 52
Indian Arts Fund
(gift of Miss Mary C. Wheelwright) T 124
Size: 36 inches by 59 inches
Colors: white, blue, madder, scarlet

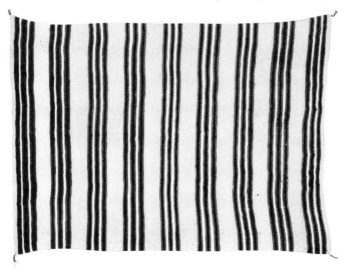

this decorative stage, the serrate style and its derivative, the rhomb, were used in this manner. In *plate 55* two serrate zigzag patterns in the bands, on either side of the central zone, may be seen, while *plate 56* demonstrates the use of an elongated mass of rhombs. A number of other pattern variations could be cited, all planned so as to bring the zone section into contrast with the background. One of these, which has resulted in an interesting effect, is a castellated treatment of the zone's edges *(plate 57)*.

There are occasions where the principle of zoning becomes greatly obscured, either because of an extreme narrowing of the section normally allotted to the background, or because of the filling of that space with decoration. When this occurs, it is obvious that such an example no longer can be classed as being zoned, but must be considered as having an all-over pattern.

Plate 53
Indian Arts Fund T 323

Size: 49 inches by 66 inches
Colors: white, black, brown, blue, dark blue, yellow, red

Plate 54
Indian Arts Fund T 193

Size: 56 inches by 61 inches
Colors: white, black, blue, red, blue-green, **57**
green-yellow, orange

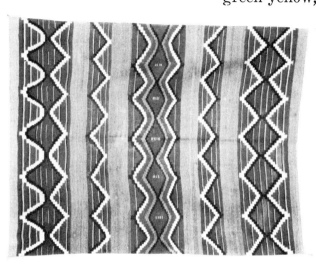

Plate 55
Indian Arts Fund T 171

Size: 51 inches by 76 inches
Colors: white, brown, grey, blue, orange,
pink, scarlet, maroon, and apricot

Plate 56
Loan: Brownell-Howland Collection
(Lab. of Anth. registered No. 260)
Size: 48½ inches by 62 inches
Colors: white, black, grey, blue, and vermilion

Plate 57
Loan: Walter R. Bimson Collection
(Lab. of Anth. registered No. 427)
Size: 52 inches by 70 inches
Colors: white, blue, black, orange, and red

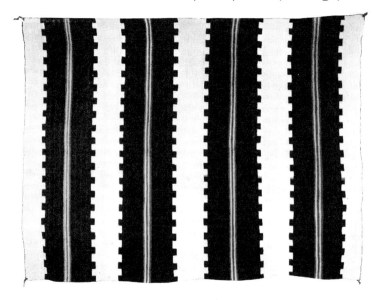

From present evidence, zoning seems to have appeared quite early in the history of Navajo weaving. In fact, it is not beyond the bounds of reason to believe that such a style had been developed by the Pueblos, from whom the Navajos received their knowledge of the craft. In support of this premise, it can be pointed out that the ever-conservative Pueblo, whose textile art-forms are known to have varied little, if any, for nearly a century and a third, still makes use of the simplest forms of zoning as a major decorative procedure.

Whether the Pueblo weaver was primarily responsible or not, the Navajo have long made use of the idea. There is a fragment of blanketry in the Laboratory of Anthropology's collection, recovered from Massacre Cave in northern Arizona where a party of these people was exterminated by the Spanish in 1805, which proves that zoning was well understood at that time.

It is interesting to note that the formal system of zoning has never lost its popularity throughout all known style-periods of Navajo blanketry, from probably as early as the late eighteenth century up to and including the present time.

9

THE OUTLINE OR
TISNASBAS BLANKET

60   AN INTERESTING and well-marked stylistic treatment in Navajo textile decoration is to be found in a class of blanketry wherein certain parts of the pattern have been outlined by narrow edgings of contrasting colors. The style apparently originated during a period in the 1890's when four-ply commercial yarns (Germantown) were being parceled out in considerable quantities to the Indians for use in weaving.

Because of the availability of a great number of colors in this kind of material, many weavers seemed determined to crowd as many of them as possible into a single fabric. Tending to further favor such a multiplicity was the use of a serrate type of design, then largely in vogue, which provided an opportunity for the inclusion of many an extra color by the outlining of the numerous zigzags, so characteristic of that style *(plate 58)*.

Later on, when the use of commercial yarn fell into disfavor with the buying public, the idea of outlining still was retained in some of the succeeding blankets and rugs woven from hand-spun, though to a lesser degree. This was particularly true for the weavers living in the vicinity of a locality called Tisnasbas, situated west of Shiprock, New Mexico. Eventually this place-name became applied to those rugs in which outlining was a prominent feature. *Plate 59* illustrates a late example.

Size: 34 inches by 54½ inches
Colors: white, black, dull purple, red, henna,
dark green, olive green, and pale salmon

61

Plate 59
Indian Arts Fund T 353

Size: 52 inches by 93 inches
Colors: grey, black, blue-black, white,
red-brown, red, orange, and yellow

10 🐐

NAVAJO TWILLED WEAVING

THE TECHNIQUE of twilled weaving was thoroughly understood by prehistoric Pueblo people at least as early as the twelfth century, and the method has continued to be used up to the present. Many examples of fabrics from pre-Columbian times attest the skill of the ancient artisan in this respect.

As the Navajos received their instruction in the art of weaving from lineal descendents of those early craftsmen, it is not at all strange that twills of various sorts appear in the textiles of that group.

Unfortunately, a lack of space permits no detailed explanation of just how the several forms of twilling are accomplished.* It may be enough for the present purpose to summarize by saying that, unlike the more familiar tapestry weave used in the majority of blankets and rugs, wherein the weft elements pass over and under every alternate warp yarn, in twilling the weft is allowed to skip one or more warps, depending on the kind of pattern desired. The simplest form of this type of weaving produces a surface with a diagonally ribbed effect, like that to be seen on the kind of cloth known as serge.

Before any weaving occurs, the various combinations of warp elements, which are to determine the type of twilled design, are attached to horizontally-placed rods called heddles. This is done so that when the heddle is pulled forward, any selected group of warp elements can be separated more easily from all the others, the weft being passed between the two divisions thus created. In addition to these heddles there is another, but unattached, rod which also functions to hold apart the warp elements

---

* Amsden, C. A.: *Navajo Weaving* contains a full description and diagrams of twilling; pp 52-57.

for the passage of the weft. This is known as the shed rod.

Three of the heddles and a shed rod, as against one of each sort used in ordinary tapestry weaving, suffice to produce a simple, diagonally-twilled fabric. The more complex the pattern, the greater the number of heddles which become necessary. In the past few years, a number of highly-skilled Navajo weavers have been able to invent patterns, in a twilled technique, of such intricacy that the use of up to sixteen heddles was demanded. One of these highly-specialized rugs, woven by Mrs. Bare Bowman of Tohatchi, New Mexico, is illustrated in *plate 65.*

Although Pueblo Indians appear always to have exhibited a marked partiality for twilling, this was not shared by the Navajo weaver until comparatively late times. In fact, this type of weaving cannot be said to have attained any noticeable degree of popularity until long after the close of the "classical" period (1850-1870) of Navajo

Plate 60
Loan: N. B. Stern (Lab. of Anth. registered No. 123)
Size: 50 inches by 76½ inches
Colors: white, blue, green, and red (raveled material)

textile industry. Since the 1880's, twilled blanketry has assumed a place of relatively greater importance, particularly as small floor rugs and saddle blankets.

The earliest piece of Navajo weaving known to the writer which demonstrates the use of a twilled technique is a blanket of the "classic" period. In this example, interrupting an otherwise unbroken expanse of tapestry weave, are narrow strips of herringbone twill, extending inward from opposite margins of the garment to a distance of about six inches *(plate 60 and detail 2)*.

Detail 2
Detail of twill weave from blanket shown on plate 60, the position of which is indicated by arrows

These must have been intended as identifying marks for either the weaver or the owner. They also prove that twilling, although seldom practiced, was not unknown to the Navajo of that time.

Plate 61 shows a saddle blanket exhibiting bands of diagonal twill, alternating in the direction of slant, and the following plate *(plate 62)*, depicts a small rug with a variety of patterns based on that method. A specimen of diamond twill or goose-eye weave is illustrated in *plate 63* and other variations appear on *plates 64 and 65*.

Plate 61
Loan: H. P. Mera

Size: 31 inches by 51½ inches
Colors: white, black, grey, and red

Plate 62
Indian Arts Fund T 222

Size: 36 inches by 60½ inches
Colors: red, green, blue, maroon, orange, and black

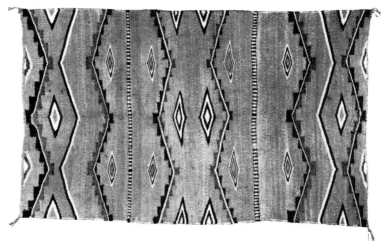

Plate 63
Indian Arts Fund T 181

Size: 26½ inches by 46 inches
Colors: white, black, and red   **67**

Plate 64
Laboratory of Anthropology $\frac{10}{488}$

Size: 28 inches by 60 inches
Colors: white, black, red, grey, and brown

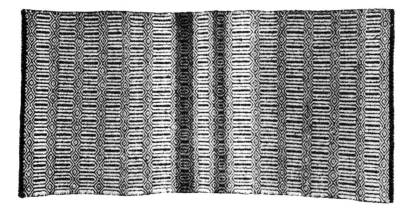

Plate 65
Indian Arts Fund T 396

68

Size: 34½ inches by 54 inches
Colors: white, black, and grey

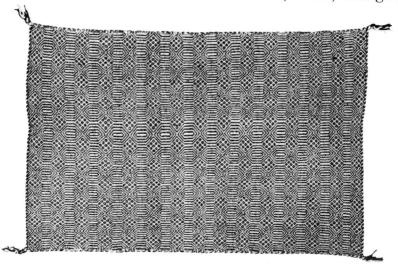

11 🐃

CLOTH-STRIP BLANKETS
OF THE NAVAJO

THERE CAN BE but little question that the least known of
the several variations in technique once employed in the
weaving of Navajo blankets is the one in which strips of
cloth, instead of yarn, were used for some of the weft elements. The cloth to be utilized for such a purpose was cut
in lengths which ranged from about one-eighth to one-half
inches in width and then were ready to be incorporated
in the weave in any one of several different ways. In every
case so far examined, some kind of flannel-like fabric had
been chosen, all previously having been dyed in the piece
with varying shades of red. Cloth strips of no other color
have been recorded in "strip" blankets.

The idea of using this type of material probably originated in a one-time custom wherein threads raveled from
an imported red cloth (bayeta) were woven into choice
blankets. This was done in order to secure more vivid
shades of that color than any obtainable from native dyes.
Later, when it was found that the superseding flannels of
domestic make could be raveled less successfully, it appears
more than likely that strips were tried out as a labor-
saving device, designed to get the same color effect without
having to separate a fabric tediously into its component
threads. Whatever the reason, this particular technique
never achieved any considerable degree of popularity.

Concerning the time when this type of weaving first
appears in the Southwest, an interesting item can be cited
in connection with the well-known saying that there is
nothing new under the sun. This adage appears to gain
some support from the finding of a fragment of cloth-
strip weave in a ruined pueblo dating from as early as

Plate 66
Recovered from a ruin in the Tonto
National Monument, Arizona

(Natural size)

Plate 67
Indian Arts Fund T 272

Size: 22 inches by 32 inches
Colors: dark red, red, dark blue, olive,
and white; fringe, grey

the fourteenth century. The bit of ancient textile which demonstrates this method is illustrated in *plate 66*. Here will be seen several short lengths of rolled, finely-woven cotton cloth which have been introduced, as a ribbed decorative feature, into a fabric otherwise comprised of a fairly coarse yarn spun from yucca fiber. As this specimen was loomed some three hundred years before the Navajos are known to have acquired the art of weaving, no possibility of a continuity of any traditional procedure can be assumed. Coming down once more to historic times, none of the Navajo "strip" blankets so far seen give any evidence of dating earlier than the middle of the 1870's nor much later than in the following decade.

Strips, as a material for weaving, are to be found in both tapestry and twilled weaves. An example of saddle-cover size, showing the latter technique, is figured in *plate 67*. As might be expected, such narrow lengths of

Plate 68
Indian Arts Fund T 410

Size: 58 inches by 74 inches
Colors: red, blue, and white

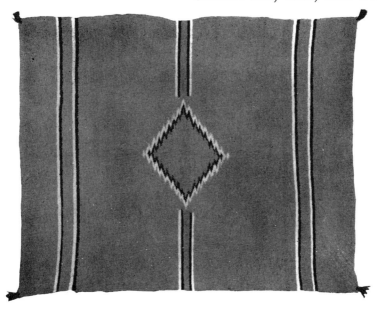

cloth, no matter how carefully prepared, could not be depended upon to lend themselves successfully to the niceties of figured design. As a consequence, yarn, usually coarsely-spun by hand to a size commensurate with the strips to be used, is never entirely missing from blankets of this class. Such yarns, aside from going into decorative units, also occur in simple stripes and bands. Strip weaving likewise is normally confined to the two latter features, although in one instance, with the exception of a comparatively small central design and a few narrow stripes worked in yarn, the entire background has been woven in that medium alone (plate 68).

From an examination of a number of specimens of this curious textile type, it has been found that there were four more or less distinct ways in which cloth strips have been utilized in the manufacture of Navajo blanketry:

1. In the simplest of the four methods, strips, just as

Plate 69
Laboratory of Anthropology $\frac{10}{405}$
Size: 46 inches by 68 inches
Colors: red, dark blue, blue-green, yellow, and white

they had been cut from the cloth, were merely woven into the fabric without regard to whether some slight twisting might take place *(plate 68)*.

2. At times, strips will exhibit a noticeable fringing along their severed edges, the result of a protusion of the cross-threads. Whether this fringing always was purposeful cannot be determined now, though in some cases it certainly appears to have been intentional. Such fringed edges, when woven, tend to produce a surface with a kind of nap or pile. *Plate 69* illustrates an example which has napped bands crossing the field at regular intervals. Both this and the previous method often result in an appearance somewhat reminiscent of a rag rug.

3. A third treatment calls for the forming of strips into rolls before weaving. Blankets of this sort may appear superficially to be woven entirely of some sort

Plate 70
Indian Arts Fund T 191

Size: 45 inches by 72 inches
Colors: red, dark blue, green, and grey

of coarse yarn. One of this type is shown in *plate 70*.

4. Although not strictly classifiable under the term "strip weaving," there is another and related process which primarily requires the cutting of cloth into strips. After this has been done, all of the short crossthreads are intended to be removed, though in practise some of these are apt to be left in place. The remaining bundle of thread elements then is used as a multiple-ply yarn. There are seldom less than five threads to the bundle, but more often that number is considerably exceeded. An example may be seen in *plate 71*. As "strip" blankets rarely present a particularly attractive appearance, only a few seem to have found their way into the hands of collectors, hence the very limited number which have been preserved can be regarded as rarities of no mean order.

Plate 71
Indian Arts Fund T 77

Size: 45 inches by 66 inches
Colors: dark red, pink, dark blue, light blue, yellow, grey, and black

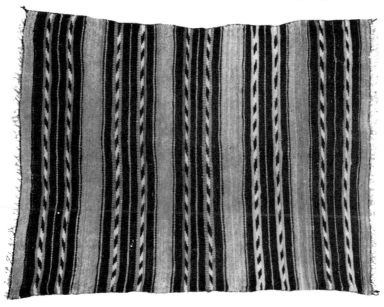

12 🐐

CHILDREN'S SHAWLS AND
SADDLE BLANKETS

HERETOFORE interest has been centered principally on matters pertaining to style, technique, or period; but in the present instance function becomes paramount. Any classification for this group, as a whole, and based on previously-used criteria, is not feasible; practically every period of style and technique in weaving is represented, the single feature common to all being a similarity in size. Blankets upon which saddles were intended to rest, as well as those designed for children's wear, all come within the dimensions characteristic of the group.

Quality is the only possible means for determining an intended use for one of these small textile forms. Even then, the exact function of some examples may remain an open question. A very general rule to follow is to class the finer weaves, those which tend to drape naturally, as probable garments, whereas others showing coarse or hard types of weaving more likely would be intended for use beneath a saddle. In many cases, it is possible approximately to date a given specimen because both the kind of material employed and the character of design closely follow the stylistic trends of the larger sizes.

Plate 72 illustrates a textile from the "classic" period (circa 1850-1875) in which raveled red cloth (bayeta) has been incorporated, in part. Other members of this group are shown in *plates 73, 74 and 75.*

Plate 72

Laboratory of Anthropology $\frac{10}{2538}$

Size: 29 inches by 48 inches
Colors: white, red (bayeta), dark
blue, light blue, and ocher

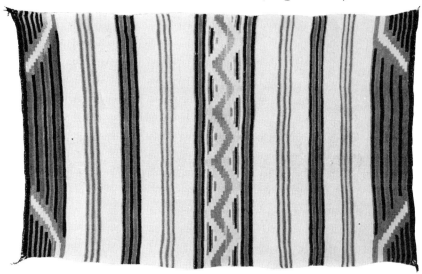

Plate 73

Laboratory of Anthropology $\frac{10}{13}$

Size: 34 inches by 51 inches
Colors: white, deep red, dark blue,
dark green, and light green

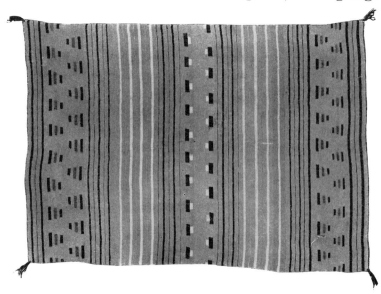

Plate 74
Laboratory of Anthropology; Stewart Collection $\frac{10}{439}$
Size: 31 inches by 49 inches
Colors: white, black, maroon, red, deep red,
dull lavender, pale green, and old gold

Plate 75
Laboratory of Anthropology; Stewart Collection $\frac{10}{436}$
Size: 31 inches by 37 inches
Colors: white, deep blue, red, lake red, and dark green

13 🐗

SADDLE COVERS

78 ANOTHER distinctive category, made up of yet smaller forms of Navajo loom-work, is to be seen in the saddle covers or "throws," as they have been called occasionally. The members of this class were used on the seats of saddles, either for some slight cushioning effect or, quite as likely, as an added item of decoration. As in the group of textiles described in the preceding section, a variety of technical methods and periods of style are represented. Besides the more usual tapestry weaves, techniques of cloth-strip, twilling and tufting are not uncommon. An unusual specimen possessing features of both cloth-strip work and twilling is shown in *plate 67*. Most saddle covers are woven so that the warp elements on one side are planned to extend for some distance beyond the fabric in order to form a fringe.

Dealers frequently speak of specimens of this sort as single saddle blankets, but their small size seems to dispose of the probability of any such use.

Three examples appear in *plates 76, 77 and 78*. The first of these was purchased in the early 1870's; the next in order is somewhat later in style; while the last is unusual because it was woven of single plies of some commercial multiple-plied yarn which had been divided expressly for that purpose.

Plate 76
Laboratory of Anthropology; Stewart Collection $\frac{10}{446}$

Size: 24 inches by 29 inches

Colors: white, light blue, dark blue, deep red, scarlet, and old gold

Plate 77
Laboratory of Anthropology $\frac{10}{455}$

Size: 27 inches by 34 inches

Colors: white, blue, light green, lavender, and yellow

Plate 78

Indian Arts Fund; Austin Collection T 419

Size: 25 inches by 28¾ inches

Colors: white, deep blue, red, light green, pale lavender, and dull yellow

Plate 79

Indian Arts Fund; Austin Collection T 393

Size: 31 inches by 53½ inches

Colors: white, grey, black, red, and brown

14 🐐

MISCELLANEOUS BLANKETRY

THERE ARE some aspects of Navajo weaving which will require only brief mention. This is because they are of more particular interest to the specialist and seldom come to the attention of the average individual.

Probably the best known of this varied assortment is the two-faced rug, so woven that each face bears a design entirely different from the other. Detailed information on how this is accomplished is too lengthy to be taken up here but may be found in Amsden's Navaho Weaving.

Somewhat allied to this, technically, is an exceedingly rare form, the double-cloth type. That is one wherein the faces, in part, are separable from one another, with something of an open space between. *Plate 79* shows an example possessing features embodying both the two-face and double-cloth methods of weaving.

Also deserving at least passing mention are the rather unattractive tufted blankets, a coarsely-woven kind in which multiple strands of long-fibred Angora goat or sheep wool are incorporated during weaving, thus giving one surface of the textile a rough-shaggy effect. Such a method at times has been utilized in the fabrication of saddle covers.

Another seldom-noticed variety is the carpet yarn rug. A number of this variant were made, circa 1900, when a short-lived attempt was made by certain traders to introduce a harsh and hairy sort of commercial, four-ply yarn. Fortunately, the movement proved unsuccessful.

Other minor oddities in Navajo loom-work have come to light from time to time, but as most of these can be viewed only as individual vagaries and had no lasting effect on the course of the craft, little is to be gained in discussing them at this time.

15 🐃

NAVAJO RUGS OF THE
CRYSTAL AND TWO GRAY
HILLS TYPES

82 THE STORY of how a White man succeeded in making drastic changes in the character of Navajo design provides an interesting chapter in the history of the textiles of that tribe.

These alterations were introduced during the last decade of the nineteenth century, when weaving, for the most part, had reached a very low ebb in all its technical aspects. The industry, at that time, had changed long since from the weaving of anything suitable for wearing apparel to an article best described as a coarse rug. A few years previous to this, a revival of "classic" decorative style fostered by Lorenzo Hubbell and C. N. Cotton at Ganado, Arizona, appears to have had no widespread or lasting beneficial effect on the quality of either spinning or weaving.

About the year 1897, J. B. Moore began operating a trading post at Crystal, New Mexico, situated west of the Chuska mountains. At this period the products of Indian looms were, for the most part, sold by the pound and at figures based on current prices of wool. His experience soon brought a realization that, under the prevailing conditions, neither the trader nor the weaver was profiting to the fullest possible extent. In consequence, he began to cast about for some means to remedy the situation. One solution seemed to lie in a greatly-improved product which might be expected to command a higher price.

After years of effort, he was able to convince the weavers in his district that rugs woven from well-spun yarns, made from a thoroughly-cleaned wool, could be disposed of at a premium. Not only was technique improved greatly but attempts were made to introduce designs more attractive to a class of purchasers not previously interested.

His accomplishments along the latter line resulted in a system of decoration quite dissimilar to, or at best, retaining only vestiges of, anything previously used by the Navajo. This breaking away from traditional forms was accomplished by means of designs made up especially for Moore's weavers. Some of these are believed, on good authority, to have been invented by Moore himself; others, it is said, are attributable to an artist friend. That this new style, despite its alien origin, became firmly established is made evident in a catalogue, illustrated in color and dated 1911, wherein a number of weavers are credited by name with designing the various examples figured.

It must not be thought that "Crystal" designs, because

Plate 80

Laboratory of Anthropology; Stewart Collection $\frac{10}{2574}$
Stewart Collection

Size: 60 inches by 100 inches
Colors: white and brown

of their unusual character, are purely inventions. Some of the standard Navajo elements always are included. It must be admitted, however, that their arrangements frequently fail to follow common usage. In the earlier examples, decoration is not far removed from Navajoan ideas *(plate 80)*. Later, elements which obviously are inventions (such as rectangular and rhomboidal hook-like figures, swastikas, frets and the like) assume increasing importance *(plates 81, 82 and 83)*. Another characteristic feature is a border enclosing the principal field of decoration. These borders either were plain or might include linear and running decorative devices.

Attention was given also to color-schemes, and although shades of red were used to a considerable extent, there was a decided tendency to feature gray, brown, and white, probably as more apt to suit the Whiteman's tastes. In the end, the "Crystal" rug became generally acknowledged as a superior article technically, if not always in the esthetic sense. A few years after the issuance of his catalogue, Mr. Moore retired from business.

Plate 81
Loan: Mr. Walter B. Kolbo
(Lab. of Anth. registered No. 586)

Size: 45½ inches by 83 inches
Colors: blue-black, white, grey, tan, and red

Plate 82
Loan: H. P. Mera

Size: 40 inches by 61 inches
Colors: black, white, grey, and tan   **85**

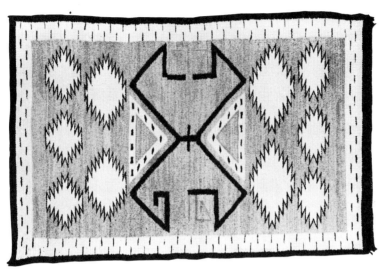

Plate 83
Loan: H. P. Mera

Size: 30 inches by 63 inches
Colors: black, white, and grey

Plate 84
Loan: H. P. Mera

Size: 52 inches by 77 inches
Colors: black, white, grey, and tan

Plate 85
Indian Arts Fund T 68

Size: 56 inches by 95 inches
Colors: black, white, grey, and brown

The next step in this curious development took place, not in the vicinity of Crystal, where it might be expected, but at a locality across the mountains, on the eastern side of the Chuskas. This situation was the result of a trans- ference of the "Crystal" idea to another setting by a man who at one time was associated with the originator.

At the new location, locally called Two Gray Hills, another distinctive style evolved, based on Crystal designs and known (after the place of its origin) as the Two Gray Hills rug. From a purely technical standpoint these rugs generally average somewhat higher than the directly ancestral type.

It is in the matter of patterns, however, that the greatest differences are to be seen. The weavers at this place, though accepting Crystal fashions in principle, have through exaggerations of earlier units of design and still further elaboration, produced effects that are unique in that they bear no close resemblance to any other textile art forms.

Another marked Two Gray Hills change is seen in the trend even farther away from the traditional use of bright colors than was true in "Crystal" rugs. This has almost wholly restricted this later class to the use of black, white, grays, and tans *(plates 84 and 85)*.

The textile art, like silversmithing, is an instance where the Navajo has taken over an idea largely alien and from it has evolved something peculiarly his own.

16 🐐

THE CHINLEE RUG

THE LATEST chapter to be written in the history of Navajo weaving is concerned with a very distinctive development. This is distinguished, not by any particular alteration in respect to design or technique, but by the use of a color-scheme which differs radically from any employed previously in the textile art of that tribe.

As this style has been in existence long enough to prove that it has successfully passed the experimental stage and now is firmly established, an account of its origin and determining characteristics should be of interest.

Following the introduction of aniline dyes in the late 1870's, the resulting colors, when used in weaving, were thought by a large number of the purchasing public to be too garish and discordant for use in the average home. An attempt to obviate this fault, previous to the appearance of the Chinlee rug, gave rise to the Two Gray Hills type which, although an improvement in some ways, was felt by many to be too austere because, as a rule, black, white, gray, and tan were employed largely to the exclusion of any of the brighter hues.

There appeared to be no middle choice for the average individual who disliked both the cold effects of one and an overgaudiness in the other, the only recourse lying in a search for old, used aniline-dyed examples in which the colors had become toned down through many washings and much exposure to light. The market for textiles of this sort of course was very restricted. This was the situation before the appearance of the Chinlee type of rug with its less vivid coloring and pleasing pastel shades, largely the result of a utilization of native vegetal dyestuffs.

Dyes of native make appear to have become largely

obsolete after commercial coloring-matter first became available, though it is quite evident from present results that the Navajo had succeeded in retaining a knowledge of many of the plants yielding them, and knowledge of their preparation. It may well be that, in the beginning, when some article was woven especially for sale or trade, a weaver from her own standpoint felt that it would be more salable and have greater attractiveness if, instead of domestic dyes of less brilliancy, the brighter-hued and more costly commercial coloring were used. And when, as time went on, the weaving of rugs became more and more important economically, it is quite to be expected that the easily-prepared aniline pigments eventually would replace the more laboriously-acquired native sort.

The genesis of the Chinlee style *(plates 86-90)* was the result of a collaborative arrangement between Mr. L. H. (Cozy) McSparron and Miss Mary Cabot Wheelwright, who sought some means to improve and popu-

Plate 86
Indian Arts Fund T 207

Size: 57 inches by 95 inches
Colors: white, black, ocher, dull orange,
pale raw umber, and dull pink

Plate 87
Indian Arts Fund T 350

Size: 42 inches by 62½ inches
Colors: white, black, grey, henna, pale
greenish yellow, and sepia

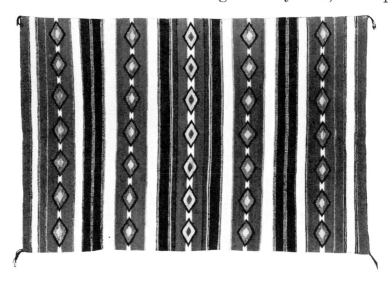

Plate 88
Laboratory of Anthropology $\frac{10}{2921}$

Size: 40 inches by 61 inches
Colors: white, black, olivaceous yellow, and rose tan

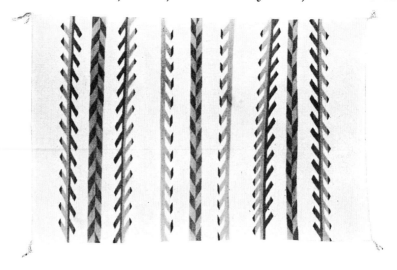

Plate 89

Laboratory of Anthropology (gift of Kinteel Trading Post)

$\frac{10}{2920}$

Size: 37 inches by 64 inches
Colors: white, black, grey, olivaceous
tan, and deep Indian red

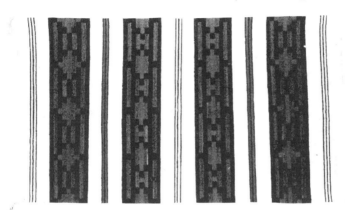

Plate 90

Laboratory of Anthropology (gift of Kinteel Trading Post)

$\frac{10}{2922}$

Size: 38½ inches by 63 inches
Colors: white, black, grey, dull rose,
raw sienna, and pale olive green

larize Navajo textile art. One of the collaborators, Mr. McSparron, has operated a trading post at Chinlee, Arizona, for many years, while Miss Wheelwright, at the time, had become greatly interested in the economic status of the weaver. Experiments embodying the new idea started as early as the first part of the 1920s. At first confined to the Chinlee district, the style has spread to many other parts of the Navajo reservation.

While the success of the revival of native dyes hung in the balance, Miss Wheelwright became instrumental in an approach to the nationally known Du Pont chemical corporation and succeeded eventually in inducing that organization to make up a number of easily-handled dyestuffs in shades intended to duplicate those seen in the old, faded, and mellowed blankets of a bygone time. Rugs in which both these dyes and the native kinds have been used in combination often are to be seen, though usually the colors deriving from vegetal substances predominate. In order to distinguish purely vegetal-dyed rugs from those having a preponderance of the new commercial coloring, the latter often are called Du Pont rugs *(plate 91)* by the trade.

Chinlee rugs are recognized readily by the color schemes, which normally include various shades of yellows and browns; warm or greenish grays; dull lake and brownish reds and a subdued pink, besides pastel shades of some of the more usual colors. At present, more than thirty-five different plant forms have yielded practical dyestuffs, the majority, however, running to shades of yellow. But despite a greatly changed appearance due to the introduction of a new idea in coloration, the structural characteristics of typical Navajo design have undergone little alteration.

Plate 91
Loan: Clay Lockett

Size: 57 inches by 81 inches
Colors: coral red, blue, and black   93

17

NAVAJO WOVEN DRESSES

Notwithstanding that it is an authoritatively-recognized fact that the Navajo Indians received their knowledge of loom-work from the Pueblos early in the eighteenth century, this must not be taken to mean that they also accepted all of the various forms of apparel to which their instructors previously had applied the art. That they did not is plainly evident in the character of the Navajo woman's dress, which differs radically from the corresponding garment traditionally worn by her village-dwelling sisters.

Whereas the native Pueblo dress consists of a single piece of fabric oblong-rectangular in shape, designed to be wrapped about the body with the greatest length extending horizontally, the old-time Navajo article was woven in two separate sections, one each for back and front, both being intended to be worn with the long axis perpendicular. Although the general shape of any single section of one of the latter of these garments offers a close resemblance to the Puebloan form, there is a technical detail in weaving which will serve to distinguish between the two. In Pueblo work the warp runs parallel to the narrower side of the dress, while the Navajo woman wove hers with that feature running lengthwise of the fabric.

For use as a dress, the short dimensions at one end of two sections were fastened together along their margins, in from the outer corners to a distance equalling the width of the shoulders, an opening being left in the center to admit the head. The result of all this was a sleeveless, tabard-like garment more or less open at the sides (*plate 92*) but which, when gathered in by a belt about the waist, actually showed very little lateral gaping. Nevertheless, there is evidence to show that at times one side or both sides were permanently sewed together, at least for a portion of their lengths.

At first thought it may seem peculiar that when weaving was taken over from the Pueblos, their style of woman's dress was not adopted as well, particularly as other textile forms made by those people were accepted, apparently without question. An explanation may lie in the mere fact that the Pueblo one-piece garment represented too great a break with established Navajo usage. In this connection, it appears safe to postulate that previous to the advent of the loom, the members of the Navajo tribe, like many others lacking a developed textile tradition, were accustomed to manufacture much of their

Plate 92

clothing from dressed animal hides, such as buckskin.

Still pursuing this line of thought, attention is called to the fact that in the making of the simpler models of Indian women's leathern dresses two hides usually were deemed necessary, one for the front, the other for the back portion. That a garment having this structural character was known to the ancient Navajo is corroborated by the description of a two-piece dress of cedar bast which occurs in a legend of that tribe. This, although not made of leather, at least tends to confirm the use of a garment of such a type in very early times. With this in

Plate 93

mind, it does not seem at all unreasonable to believe that the Navajo woman preferred to continue the old two-piece fashion, merely exchanging buckskin or bast for a woven woolen fabric *(plate 93)*.

The type of loom and the technique employed depart but little from those customarily used by the other aboriginal weavers of the Southwest. In the weaving of these dresses, a simple tapestry method was maintained throughout, like that seen in the average Indian blanket, in which the weft completely hides the warp elements. But aside from such similarities, the Navajo dress presents an appearance to the eye which is strikingly different from any other native product fabricated in that area. From a technical standpoint the only difference in the process of weaving this garment which deviates in any way from that employed in ordinary blanketry is that the two patterned ends were woven first, the whole of the dark-colored central portion being filled in afterward.

For the sake of description, each individual half of one of these garments may be said to be divisible into three sections, a central one and two ornamental bands extending across the ends at top and bottom. The first of these divisions, as far as is known, always is woven from either a wool yarn dyed black or a similar material having a more brownish cast, obtained from so-called black sheep. The various designs to be seen in the patterned bands illustrate the greatest degree of differentiation attempted from an otherwise strictly maintained, standardized treatment.

In early times, credible tradition has it that, at first, decorative devices consisted solely of a number of indigo stripes running transversely across the ends. Unfortunately, none of this sort appears to have survived the ravages of time, though a single example is known to exist which closely approaches that style, only differing by having the blue stripes narrowly outlined in red *(plate 94)*. Decorative fashions of a later period called for large areas of red to form a background, other colors being relegated to subordinate and less conspicuous details. *Plates 94, 95 and 96* figure a representative sampling of decorative bands. Still other and different designs may be seen in *plates 92 and 93*.

Normally, all of the blue and black yarns going into these garments will be found to have been spun by hand while the reds, greens and yellows seldom were. A material obtained from the raveled red cloth called bayeta, occurring in many of the older examples, was replaced by shredded flannel, carded and respun, in those dating from a later period. Various machine-spun yarns of green and yellow on occasion were used for some of

Plate 94

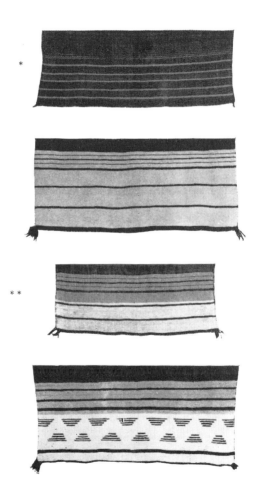

the minor features of a pattern. *Plate 96* (see marginal *) illustrates the use of a commercial green yarn, which for the purposes of weaving had been separated into its component plies, in a stripe at the top of the band, as well as for a staggered row of rectangles near the bottom. One ingenious weaver in the past combined threads of red bayeta with ravelings of some sort of yellow material to produce the effect shown on the lower part of the band seen in *plate 94* (see ** on margin).

Hand-woven dresses of the kind here discussed apparently were worn from sometime early in the eighteenth century until as late as the first part of the 1890's, though

Plate 95

they become progressively less common toward the end of the period. After that date they went entirely out of fashion, and were superseded by the velvet blouses and voluminous skirts now in vogue.

Plate 96

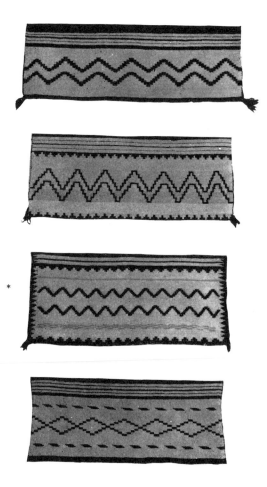

18

WHAT DOES THE
FUTURE HOLD?

THE PRECEDING pages describe and illustrate the principal features of Navajo weaving, from about the beginning of the nineteenth century up to circa 1940.

What the future may hold for the craft is, of course,
purely conjectural, although certain possibilities of things
to come are not entirely lacking. One of these is the
eventual substitution of the wage-hour idea of compen-
sation for a long established system of barter. What with
the Navajo becoming more and more familiar with indus-
trial conditions at large, an attempt at such a change is
not at all beyond belief.

Up to recent times, both the weaver and the trader
have found that barter has proved the most practical
way for dealing with one another, inasmuch as most of
the loom-work has had to be accomplished in the intervals between routine domestic duties, often with some
time spent in herding the family flock. Under such conditions, attempts to introduce a strict observance of the
time element would give rise to many misunderstandings
and difficult situations throughout the industry. All this
could easily lead to a serious falling off in the rate of
production with resulting losses of revenue to the Indians.

Following a similar line of thought, another factor
came to light during an experiment in weaving which
took place several years ago. In this, some experienced
weavers were relieved of all other duties, housed at a
government school and paid an hourly wage equal to that
earned by unskilled labor in prewar years. With a nom-
inal overhead and cost of material charged against the
work, results proved that the rugs woven by these women

were found to cost several times more than the prices asked by their more leisurely working sisters on the reservation.

Should the wage-hour system be widely adopted by the Navajo, thus greatly increasing the market value of rugs, there can be little doubt but that the number of buyers would be seriously lessened, particularly as a majority of the tourist trade is inclined to view the Navajo rug as a "curio" instead of a practical and durable floor covering. Still another unfortunate situation could develop from the production of a poorly woven, sleazy article in order to reduce the cost. This would most assuredly react adversely on the future of Navajo textile art.

Time alone will tell the outcome.

▲ ▲ This edition of

NAVAJO TEXTILE ARTS

has been designed in the bold simplicity of Indian Crafts by

MERLE ARMITAGE

AFTERWORD

FORTUNATELY H. P. Mera was a much better historian than fortune-teller, and the rather doleful and pessimistic final chapter of his book, like the similarly negative projections of almost all other writers on Navajo textiles, has been refuted by the ongoing artistry and craftsmanship in succeeding generations of Navajo women. The Navajo weaver has not converted her thinking to the hourly wage concept. Like the rural women who produce traditional patchwork quilts, she still weaves in her spare time and barters or sells the finished textile on the open market or thru the Navajo Crafts Guild.

Neither has the quality of Navajo weaving declined since Mera's time to satisfy tourist demand for an inexpensive curio. Instead, a marvelous renaissance has occured in Navajo weaving, a renaissance hinted at by Mera in his chapters on Crystal, Two Gray Hills and Chinle rugs. It is true that the number of textiles being produced today is probably the lowest in this century, but this scarcity in the face of a growing demand for the work has enabled Navajo weavers to increase the prices charged for rugs. The increase in the cost of first-quality Navajo weaving has at once allowed the weaver to earn a more realistic income and redefined the market for her work. Although small and inexpensive throws and saddle-blanket sized rugs are still being produced for the curio seeker (imitation-Navajo rugs are being imported from Mexico for this market as well), the best of today's weaving—which ranks with the very finest Navajo weaving of the past, even of the Classic Period—is being sold to serious collectors who can pay the high prices of today's market and in return demand a level of perfection until recently undreamed of. Thus the increased income for the weaver and the increased sophistication of the consumer have worked together to produce contemporary Navajo textiles which both in technical virtuosity and in aesthetic quality can only be called "Neoclassic." That weavers are now recognized by name is an indication of the transition from craft to art. The quantity of new rugs has vastly declined since Mera's day, but the quality has seen a marked rise, and the art of Navajo weaving has never been healthier.

THE purpose of this Afterword is to comment briefly on Mera's book in light of present knowledge and to trace briefly the renaissance in Navajo weaving which has taken place since the book was written.[1] Thus it appears as a series of short, independent commentaries on the book, and is arranged in roughly the same order as the book itself.

MERA'S INTRODUCTORY ESSAY

Both of the major writings on Navajo textiles which were written between the two World Wars—the present volume and Amsden's *Navaho Weaving, Its Technic and History*—discuss Saxony yarn, the three-ply, European manufactured yarn which was popular with Navajo weavers during and after their confinement in the concentration camp of Bosque Redondo in the late 1860s. Both also mention the elusive "Zephyr" yarn. The term "Zephyr" has never been adequately defined and is no longer in current usage. If it ever had a precise meaning, it is now long lost.

CHAPTER ONE

There is little to be added to Mera's chapter on the so-called "Chief Blanket" except to note that today the woman's shoulder blankets *(plates 7-10)* are thought of as a unique category of weaving separate from the "Chief Blanket," and that the latter is now divided into identifiable phases. Phase I is illustrated in *plate 2*, Phase II is shown in *plates 3 and 4*, and Phase III is shown in *plates 5 and A (endsheet)*. For a more complete discussion of the phases of "Chief Blanket" patterning see Maxwell's *Navajo Rugs: Past, Present & Future*. Later textiles using design elements of the "Chief Blanket" are not blankets at all. Being thickly woven and intended for use as floor coverings they must more properly be called rugs *(plates 6 and B)*. A few rugs with such patterns are still being produced.

Plate B
A rug from the "Hubbell Revival Period" (ca. 1890–1910). Size: 68 inches by 79 inches. All handspun. The diamond shaped patterning is in black, red and white; banded background stripes are brown and black on the upper half of the rug and black and faded purple on the lower half. Note also the three bands of narrow white "beading."

Black, white, and brown are natural wool colors; red and purple are aniline dyed.

CHAPTER THREE

Mera's essay on the "Slave Blanket" is mainly of historical interest to today's reader, since these textiles are now exceedingly rare. It should be noted that two of Mera's means of identifying "Slave Blankets"—the existence of a braided selvage on all edges and the existence of "lazy lines"—though useful in identifying 19th Century textiles are no longer iron-clad means of recognizing the Navajo origin of more contemporary textiles. Today it is rather common to find Navajo rugs which do not have a braided edge cord running parallel to the warp, though the selvage along the warp ends of the textile invariably exists in undamaged pieces. Conversely it is today rather common to find imitation-Navajo rugs of Mexican origin which do have braided edge cords running parallel to the warp. Mexican weavers have become increasingly artful at imitating Navajo rugs in the last few years and now often include this edge cord, though it is a great deal of extra work to do so on the horizontal harness looms which they use.

It has long and almost universally been thought that the "lazy line" is unique to the upright loom used by the Navajo. It is true that this technique is much more commonly used by the Navajo than by any other weaver in the world, but it is not unique to the Navajo. True "lazy lines" (that is, diagonal weft changes which bear no relationship to the pattern of the textile) have been documented in Mayo serapes from Mexico.[2] The writers have also seen the technique employed on oriental textiles of the Kelim type and on a tapestry weaving from Scandinavia. Mera and others who argue that the production of "lazy lines" is almost impossible on a harness loom discount the degree to which finger weaving can be and is done on that type of loom. Nineteenth Century Saltillo serapes are a notable example of this. The Navajo loom is ideal for finger weaving, but it is not the only loom on which finger weaving techniques, twined edge cords, or "lazy lines" are produced.

CHAPTER FOUR

The essay on "Pictorial Blankets" neglects to mention the Yei rug, a rug which pictures a row of tall, slim characterizations of Navajo religious figures encompassed on three sides by a long, narrow rainbow-like figure *(plate C)*. For a further discussion of this kind of rug and its distinction from the Yeibichai rug illustrated in *plate 33* see Maxwell's *Navajo Rugs: Past, Present & Future.*

Plate C
Yei rug. Size: 29 inches by 51 inches. All handspun. The background is a carded gray. The Yei figures are done in vegetal tans, browns, and yellows. A bit of aniline turquoise decorates the Yei figures, and the black border is aniline dyed. Date: 1968.

CHAPTER FIVE

The revival of "classic" designs which flourished around
Hubbell's Ganado Trading Post from approximately 1890
to 1910 encouraged the reuse of many traditional designs,
including women's dresses, shoulder blanket and serrate
patterns, as well as banded background designs. Not all
of the textiles from the "Hubbell Revival Period" were
woven from Germantown yarn; many examples exist
which were woven from Navajo handspun and aniline
dyed yarn. See *plate B* for one example of a handspun
rug from that period. This rug illustrates the influence
of both the banded-background and the "Chief Blanket"
on the "Hubbell Revival" rugs. The bands of "poisonous
purple" so typical of this period have mercifully faded to
a mellow bluish-gray. Mera is quite right in calling these
textiles rugs and thus distinguishing them from earlier
banded-background blankets.

CHAPTER SIX

Any confusion the reader may feel in reading the analysis
of *plate 45* which appears on page 47 can be dispelled if
the reader will turn the illustration so that the left hand
end of the textile is viewed as its bottom and the right
hand end as the top.

CHAPTER NINE

The "Tisnasbas" blankets could also more properly be
called rugs. (Contemporary spelling of the name of this
trading post and the rugs woven around it is Teec Nos
Pos, pronounced Tēs Näs Päs.) The outline design motif
of these textiles had its roots in the late-19th Century
introduction of Germantown yarn which is associated
with late blankets and early rugs. Often these rugs en-

close the busy, multicolored outline designs that Mera describes in a wide border boldly decorated with a bright, elaborate border design. The production of these outline rugs in the Teec Nos Pos area has continued from the 1890s to the present (see *plate D*). The popularity of Germantown yarns, which ebbed in the early 1900s in most parts of the reservation, has continued unabated in and around Teec Nos Pos.[3] These rugs still often include Germantown yarn, although many textiles made entirely from handspun yarn are also produced. The common denominator for such rugs is the bold outlining in bright colors which comes from commercial aniline dyes.

Plate D
Teec Nos Pos tapestry. Size: 28 inches by 33 inches. All handspun. The background is a carded gray. Patterns are of natural white and aniline black, browns, and yellow. The slight fuzziness of the lines is caused by brushing the textile after weaving, an occasional practice among Navajo weavers. Date: 1973. Woven by Sara Begay.

Except for the tufted saddle covers which are mentioned in Chapter 13 and expanded upon in Chapter 14, the textiles which Mera calls "saddle covers" are actually single saddle blankets designed to be used under the saddle, flat on the horse's back. The saddle blankets discussed in Chapter 12 are double saddle blankets designed to be folded in half and used between the horse and the saddle. Both single and double saddle blankets are still being produced. They are usually roughly woven from a heavy, soft handspun yarn. Contemporary patterning of saddle blankets usually includes a few broad, simple stripes, with a bit of further decoration at the four corners, the only part of the blanket visible when it is in place. Less common are the thick, resilient blankets of traditional twilled weaves. However, imitation Navajo textiles from Mexico are often seen in these patterns and are sold as saddle blankets in tack shops as well as by Indian crafts dealers. The Mexican twilled reproductions can be particularly difficult to distinguish from their Navajo counterparts. Fringes of the kind Mera describes in Chapter 13 are rarely seen on contemporary saddle blankets, but their remnant—knotted warp ends at one end of the textile—are still common. This knotted warp end (usually concealed by a false end selvage) often occurs because a weaver has woven two saddle blankets on the same loom, cut the two apart in the middle, and knotted up the loose warp ends on both pieces. This technique is almost universal in the Mexican imitations and is also very common in Gallup throws, the small Navajo weavings designed for tourists who want inexpensive Navajo curios.

CHAPTER FOURTEEN

Mera shares the general view that the tufted blankets (or saddle covers) are unattractive and coarsely-woven. There

are traders who refuse to handle such weavings. It is true that these blankets are often crude and are not very important to the mainstream of Navajo weaving. But, at their best, they do have a certain charm, and it would be unfortunate if the *only* example of piled weaving in the history of the craft should be driven into extinction because of the prejudice of traders and scholars—the very people who should encourage diversity and creativity in traditional craft practices.

In addition to the miscellaneous blanketry which Mera discusses, some passing reference should be made to other Navajo textile arts which do not involve the standard, upright Navajo loom.

The Navajo have long woven and continue to weave sashes which, in technique and design, are much like those of the Pueblo people and intended for use as belts. These sashes are woven on long narrow belt-looms and the patterning is produced by exposing the warp on part of the face of the textile. Both handspun and Germantown yarns are used. The colors and patterning of *plate E*—red background with two narrow bands of green weft and white warp exposed to create triangular patterns on the front; a simple red and white stripe on the back—are typical of Navajo sashes.

Another form of Navajo textile is the man's leggings. These leggings are knitted, usually by and for men. They are almost always black or dark blue and are unpatterned except for a ridge or two running up the outside. The Navajo also have a tradition of producing woven men's shirts and saddle girths.

Additionally it might be mentioned that the Navajo also weave basketry of a utilitarian nature, including pitched water bottles.

CHAPTERS EIGHT, FIFTEEN, AND SIXTEEN

Mera's essays on Zoning Treatment, Crystal, Two Gray Hills, and Chinlee (contemporary spelling is Chinle) rugs should be discussed together since they collectively describe some of the roots of the contemporary "Neoclassic" textiles which were mentioned earlier.

The somber and beautiful Two Gray Hills rug from western New Mexico is the best known and most technically superior textile ever to emerge from the Navajo loom. Developed by traders in that area during the second decade of the 20th Century, the Two Gray Hills rug (or tapestry as many should now be called) relies almost exclusively on undyed sheep colors: brown, white, black (actually a deep, rich brown), grays and tans which come either from natural sheep colors or from carding black and white wool together before spinning. Today natural black wool is almost always enhanced by dying with an aniline black. Brown dyes are also sometimes used to enhance the sheep browns. The patterning usually involves one or more very ornate diamond shaped medallions set on a background of brown or gray which is enclosed by two or more ornate borders. When the style using these colors and patterns first appeared, the weavers of Two Gray Hills textiles were producing good heavy floor rugs designed to compete both in pattern and wearability with the oriental rugs of the day. Today the Two Gray Hills tapestry is much smaller and finer; too fine to use as a floor rug, it is really intended as a piece for display as a wall hanging or "woven painting" (see *plate F*).

Plate F
Two Gray Hills tapestry. Size: 29 inches by 46 inches. All handspun. Colors: natural black, white, brown, carded gray, and tan. Black has been enhanced with an aniline dye. Date: 1973. Woven by Dorine Gould.

Among the contemporary criteria for judging the quality of a Navajo textile are the fineness of warp and weft, the closeness of the warp threads to each other, the tightness with which the weft has been packed, the skill with which yarns have been dyed, carded or matched, and the ability of the weaver to make a truly rectangular piece with opposite sides paralleling each other and with true ninety-degree angles at the corners.

Using any or all of these criteria, the best Two Gray Hills tapestries of today (although lacking the vigor of design and visual impact of the Classic Period blankets) are the finest textiles ever produced by Navajo weavers.

The Chinle rug which Mera saw as the latest and one of the most important evolutions in Navajo rug design is today seldom seen. Rugs colored with Du Pont chemical dyes *(plate 91* and the *cover illustration)* and Diamond "Old Navaho" dyes never gained the popularity which Mera foresaw for them and are now quite rare. And the purely vegetal-dyed rugs from the Chinle area are no finer and much scarcer than they were a decade ago.

However the pioneering efforts of L. H. McSparron and Mary Cabot Wheelwright have borne their best fruits south and east of Chinle in two areas which are now regarded as having the finest weavers working within the tradition of borderless, vegetal-dyed rugs. These are the region around Crystal, New Mexico where vegetal dyes have entirely replaced the aniline dyed "old style Crystal" rugs of the turn of the century, and the area in the southern part of the reservation around the trading posts at Pine Springs, Wide Ruins, and Burntwater, Arizona. Rugs from both of these regions have two important traits in common: the use of vegetal dyes and the "zoning" or banded treatment of design elements which Mera discusses in Chapter 8. This "zoning" can be traced in an unbroken line from the earliest known Navajo weaving to the present and is used with marvelous subtlety by the contemporary weavers of the vegetal dyed rugs from these areas.

The Crystal rug of today *(plate G)* can be distinguished from rugs of the Pine Springs-Wide Ruins-Burntwater area by the characteristic "wavy" appearance of the undecorated background on which the bands or "zones" of decoration have been 'placed. It is also quite common in Crystal rugs for this "wavy" background, or "Crystal stripe" *(plate G inset)*, to be broken into bands of alternating color combinations. The use of an elongated mass of rhombs which Mera mentions in his discussion of "zoned" rugs quite commonly defines the "zoned" bands in Crystal rugs. These rugs are normally much heavier than other vegetal dyed textiles and are perfectly serviceable as floor rugs.

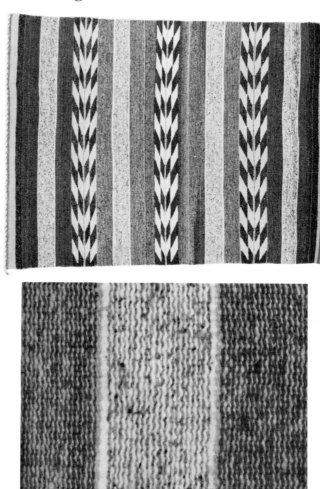

Plate G

Crystal rug. Size: 46 inches by 62 inches. All handspun. Colors: natural white and vegetal tans, gray, brown, and green. Date: 1970. Woven by Nan Bitsi.

Detail of *Plate G* illustrates the characteristic "Crystal stripe."

Textiles from the Pine Springs-Wide Ruins-Burnt-water area *(plate H, endsheet)*, like the contemporary Crystal rugs, exhibit "zoned" treatment of the design elements and, like other "zoned" rugs, are borderless. However, the "wavy" appearance of the background noted in the Crystal rug is here largely absent. Here the background is much plainer, although often decorated with very narrow bands of "beading" and "dotting" *(plate H inset)* and occasionally with very narrow bands of "Crystal stripe" used in combination with the "beading" and "dotting." The "zoned" areas of textiles from Pine Springs-Wide Ruins-Burntwater rely less on rhombs and exhibit much more imagination in the design of decorative elements, often having three or more independent or interlocking design motifs next to each other in each of the "zones." These textiles usually have three, four, or five major decorated "zones," and traders in this part of the Navajo reservation encourage weavers to make textiles with five major "zones" as well as the narrow bands of very sophisticated "beading" and "dotting" to relieve the starkness of the areas between "zones." Although the vegetal dyed textiles from this area have yet to achieve the technical perfection of the Two Gray Hills tapestries, most of them are too finely woven and subtly colored to use as floor rugs and should be considered as wall hangings. The elegant pastel colors of these tapestries are prefered by many who find the black, white, brown, and gray of Two Gray Hills textiles too austere.

The finest of contemporary Navajo tapestries from both the Two Gray Hills region and the Pine Springs-Wide Ruins-Burntwater area are sometimes produced from commercially carded "roving." The purchase of this commercial roving eliminates for the Navajo weaver the first three stages of preparing the wool for spinning: shearing, cleaning, and carding; and it gives the spinner a beautifully clean, long staple wool which can be spun and dyed with almost perfect uniformity. Some weavers also use roving of pre-carded gray or pre-dyed colors, thus further simplifying their preparations for spinning.

In closing, brief mention of some of the other contemporary products of the Navajo loom should be made.

The area around Ganado (between Chinle and Wide Ruins in Arizona) continues, in its old tradition, to produce many good floor rugs and a few excellent tapestries in black, gray, white, and red, often using a rich red produced by double-dying wool with an aniline dye *(plate I)*. The "Chapter House Rug," although not unique to this area, is often seen there. This is a rug woven communally by several women at the regional Chapter House or community meeting house, usually from commercial roving. These rugs tend to be sturdy, well woven floor rugs which lack the splendid graphic innovations so often seen in rugs woven by a single artisan.

Plate I

Ganado tapestry. Size: 41 inches by 62 inches. All handspun. The background is a deep double-dyed red characteristic of the best weaving from the Ganado area. Patterning and borders are in natural white, carded gray, and aniline dyed black. Date: 1968. Woven by Elsie Wilson.

To the west of any of the geographical areas previously discussed lies almost half of the Navajo reservation. In this region rough rugs and saddle blankets are produced in some quantity, almost always using aniline dyes and bold, geometric patterns. Rugs woven from commercial cotton "carpet yarn" and various synthetic plied yarns are also made in this area. These rugs are now filling the tourists' demand for relatively inexpensive Indian curios. Thus, this area produces the poorest examples of the Navajo textile arts, those which will probably next cease to exist, and those which will be least missed.

One important exception is the attractive and sturdy "Raised Outline" rug (*plate J*) which is produced around Coal Mine Mesa in the western reservation. The uniqueness of these rugs lies in a relatively new technique wherein changes in the pattern are accentuated by a row of weft threads which have been raised or superimposed on the body of the rug, giving it a three dimensional

Plate J

"Raised Outline" rug. Size: 28 inches by 48 inches. Warp is handspun; weft is all Germantown yarn. Colors: black, white, brown, and gold. Date: 1971. Woven by Ann Jim.

character on one face. The entire body of these rugs is woven of vertical "beaded" stripes on which the raised outline patterns are laid. The rugs are commonly woven of Germantown yarns.

Some 85 years ago Navajo weavers adapted their blankets into rugs to meet the changing consumer demand. So, today, the weaver is converting her rugs into fine tapestries of "Neoclassic" quality. Thus it would appear that the future of Navajo weaving rests primarily with a small group of highly skilled artisans in the eastern half of the reservation who are weaving artistically conceived and remarkably executed works of textile art for the increasingly sophisticated tastes of the collector.

[1]However no attempt will be made to repeat information already available in either Gilbert S. Maxwell's excellent 1963 booklet, *Navajo Rugs: Past, Present & Future*, or in Kate Peck Kent's fine 1961 booklet, *The Story of Navaho Weaving*, both of which did so much to codify a vocabulary for those interested in Navajo weaving and to identify the geographical regions which are producing uniquely patterned rugs. As Mera refers his reader to Amsden's *Navaho Weaving, Its Technic and History*, we will refer the reader to Maxwell and Kent and confine our comments to those areas not discussed by earlier writers, including changes which have occured in the years since Maxwell's booklet first appeared.

[2]See for example Ralph L. Beals, *Contemporary Culture of Cahita Indians*, (Bureau of American Ethnology Bulletin #142, 1945), page 30.

[3]Fortunately the practice of cutting and knotting the end warps, so common in turn of the century Germantowns, is no longer often seen.

APPENDIX

THE Afterword has made passing references to the imitation Navajo rugs which have been coming from Mexico in ever growing numbers in the last few years. Until recently genuine Navajo textiles were easily recognizable. Unfortunately, however, some Indian weavers of Mexico, under the pressure of commercialism, have been producing "artful" imitations of Navajo textiles which are becoming increasingly difficult to distinguish from authentic Navajo pieces. It is truly regrettable that the rich and varied textile skills of the Mexican Indian weaver should be turned to producing poor quality, soulless, rote copies of the currently fashionable Navajo rug designs. The Mexican copies can be found in a full range of Navajo patterns: double saddle blankets of either twill or simple stripes, Two Gray Hills, Crystals, Yeis, and many others. The following chart is offered to illustrate how difficult this identification can be and to give some technical information on how such identification can be accomplished.

For further information on this subject we refer the reader to Noël Bennett's excellent recent pamphlet, *Genuine Navajo Rugs—Are You Sure?*

		NAVAJO TEXTILES	MEXICAN IMITATIONS
YARNS	Handspun weft threads	Spun on a spindle, either from native wool or from commercial roving; long staple, full of natural lanolin	Spun on a spinning-wheel; short staple, soft, dry, "punky," sometimes smelling of chemicals
	Germantown weft threads	Occasionally; both wool and various synthetics	Rarely
	Warp threads	Usually wool; occasionally cotton string	Usually cotton string; occasionally wool
	Dyes	Vegetal or aniline	Usually aniline, though what appear to be vegetal dyes are now being seen
WEAVING TECHNIQUES	Type of loom	Upright	Horizontal, harness loom
	Knotted warp ends (i.e. lack of a continuous warp)	Rarely	Always; but often cleverly hidden
	Braided end selvage	Always; except on Gallup throws and some saddle blankets	Often used to hide knotted warp ends
	Doubled warp on and near the edges	Very seldom; usually in the absence of twined edge cords	Always; often several warps near the edge are doubled
	Braided edge cords	Usually	Occasionally
	Tightness of weft packing	Very firm in all but the poorest examples	Even but loose, with warp threads easily exposed
MISC.	Woven by an American Indian	Yes; usually by women	Yes; usually by boys and young men
	Patterns	Traditional or innovative	Copied; often from books on Navajo weaving
	Durability	Excellent	Poor
	Price	Some, but not all, dealers price the Mexican imitations well below the price of comparable Navajo pieces (a few even leave the "Made in Mexico" tags attached to the textiles), but Let the Buyer Beware!	

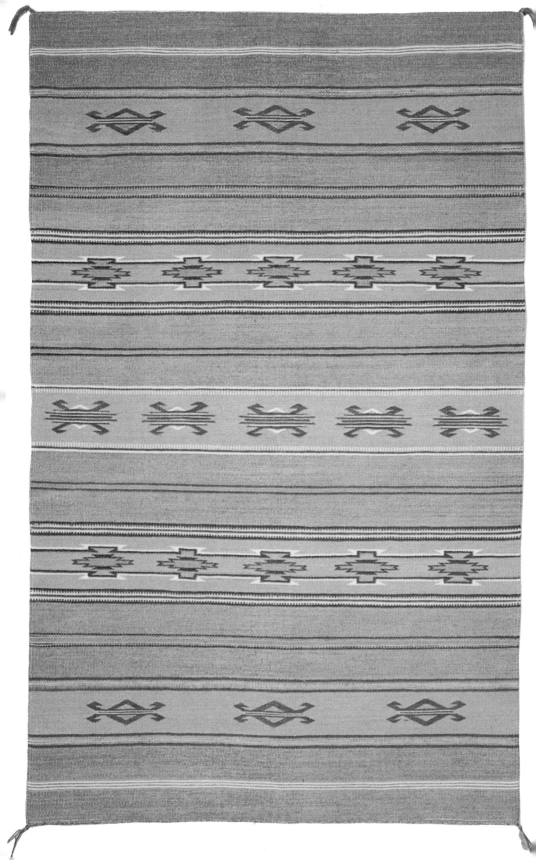